To: Dean

# EBONY TOWERS IN HIGHER EDUCATION

Tonyelli Bertrand Ricard

1-12-09

# EBONY TOWERS IN HIGHER EDUCATION

The Evolution, Mission, and Presidency of
Historically Black Colleges and Universities

*Ronyelle Bertrand Ricard and
M. Christopher Brown II*

Foreword by *Lenoar Foster*

STERLING, VIRGINIA

Sty/us

COPYRIGHT © 2008 BY STYLUS PUBLISHING, LLC.

Published by Stylus Publishing, LLC
22883 Quicksilver Drive
Sterling, Virginia 20166-2102

**Library of Congress Cataloging-in-Publication Data**
Ricard, Ronyelle Bertrand, 1977–
   Ebony towers in higher education : the evolution,
mission, and presidency of historically black colleges and
universities / Ronyelle Bertrand Ricard and M. Christopher
Brown II ; foreword by Lenoar Foster.—1st ed.
      p.   cm.
   Includes bibliographical references and index.
   ISBN 978-1-57922-273-4 (cloth : alk. paper)—ISBN 978-
1-57922-274-1 (pbk. : alk. paper)
1. African American universities and colleges.   2. African
Americans—Education (Higher)   3. African American
college presidents.   I. Brown, M. Christopher.   II. Title.
LC2781.R527   2008
378.1'982—dc22                                    2007031389

13-digit ISBN: 978-1-57922-273-4 (cloth)
13-digit ISBN: 978-1-57922-274-1 (paper)

Printed in the United States of America

All first editions printed on acid free paper that meets the
American National Standards Institute z39-48 Standard.

Bulk Purchases

Quantity discounts are available for use in workshops
and for staff development.
Call 1-800-232-0223

First Edition, 2008

10 9 8 7 6 5 4 3 2 1

To my mother, Patricia A. Bertrand—
I recognize that this body of work exists
because of your hard work and sacrifice.
Thank you for your years of love, support, and commitment.
To my husband Craig Ricard—
your love, support, and encouragement have truly sustained me.
Never forget—
Greater is NOW!!!

—rbr


To "the Family" and all of our intellectual progeny.
I celebrate the way in which we have continued to support each other,
created our own frameworks for success, and mentored a
new generation of scholars committed to community scholarship.
This work exemplifies our greatest aim of passing on
the legacy—"each one reach one."
I honor the memory of the late Dr. Clinton Bristow, Jr.—
who served as the intellectual motivation for this book.
My late grandmother, Mrs. Evelyna S. Brown, used to say,
"Heap see, but few know."

—mcb2

Historically black colleges and universities play a critical role in American higher education. They produce a disproportionate number of African American baccalaureate recipients and are the undergraduate degree of origin for a disproportionate share of Ph.D.s to blacks. These institutions perform miracles in elevating disadvantaged youth to productive citizenship. **If they did not exist, we would have to invent them.**

—William H. Gray, III
*Former President, United Negro College Fund*

# CONTENTS

An important and contemporary aggregate of effectiveness for institutions of higher education in the United States is the degree to which graduates have attained academic, social, economic, and political readiness for a society that is increasingly multicultural and global. Accreditation bodies have enjoined American higher education institutions to evaluate the success of their students and graduates against mission statements and leadership direction that clearly delineate institutional prioritization of resources and strategic planning. In short, when institutional benchmarks of mission, teaching, research, and service are supported by an infrastructure of leadership and dedicated resources, students mirror the success of colleges and universities from which they have graduated through a number of quantifiable measures. Among these measures are the rank and caliber of the graduate schools to which they have been accepted; the internship and job opportunities they have garnered at Fortune 500 and other top-ranked business conglomerates; the notoriety of their post-graduate accomplishments; the importance and significance of the corridors of power through which they have become associated as a result of their talent, achievement, and political, social, and economic affiliation; and, the innovations and contributions they are positioned to make in a variety of endeavors because they simply possess the educational credentials and tools for both leadership and service. For substantial numbers of African American college graduates, Historically Black Colleges and Universities (HBCUs) have provided the gateway and means for them to achieve and prosper within these measures of success. While constituting only about 3 percent of the institutions of higher education in the United States, HBCU institutions enroll 14 percent of African American undergraduates and they graduate 28 percent of all African Americans who earn an undergraduate degree, a graduation rate higher than for African American students who attend predominantly White institutions. Over 50 percent of African American professionals are graduates of HBCU institutions; over 50 percent of African American public school teachers and 70 percent of African American dentists secured their professional and pre-professional training at HBCU institutions. Fifty percent of African Americans who graduate from HBCU institutions pursue advanced study in graduate and professional schools. Half of the degrees held by African Americans in mathematics are awarded by HBCU institutions, and these institutions award more than one in three of the degrees awarded to African Americans in the natural sciences (United Negro College Fund, 2007). And, these institutions continue to do so today amid continuing, incessant, and unrelenting analysis and reconsideration of their mission, role, and status in American higher education. Willie, Reddick, and Brown (2006) note, "Black colleges are a classic illustration of being damned if you do and damned if you don't. For Black colleges and universities, antinomies appear to be eternal" (p.23).

There is a running anecdotal commentary among many Black professors who teach in graduate programs at predominantly White higher education institutions in this country that you can distinguish the Black students who come from undergraduate HBCU institutions to study in White graduate schools from those Black students who come from predominantly White undergraduate institutions to study at similar institutions. As the commentary goes, HBCU students appear more poised and confident. Their resilience to institutional practices and barriers that seek to minimize their training and their status is far greater than that of their Black peers who have attended predominantly White colleges and universities. This resilience appears to be born of an "institutional mission-effectiveness" that appears to have pervaded their educational, leadership, and service experiences at HBCU institutions. Importantly, these HBCU graduates in predominantly White environs continue to enjoy the support and encouragement of administrators (presidents, vice presidents, provosts, deans), academic officers (department chairs, academic advisers, etc.), faculty, and staff members from their HBCU alma maters who follow their progress and provide focus for their continuing work and progress. When asked why this support continues and is so important and valued, these Black graduate students from HBCU institutions often remark that this type of continuing support has always been part and parcel of the "central mission" of their educational experience. That is, their educational experience has been framed by an institutional leadership and strategic alignment that have promoted and laid the groundwork for student engagement and success. And what appears to be so powerful about this legacy from HBCU graduates is that they have been privy to this guidance and nurturance from role models who have been successful themselves in attaining advanced graduate degrees. All of this anecdotal observation of HBCU graduates stands in stark comparison to the educational experiences of Black students who are graduates of predominantly White institutions. These Black students often recount living and learning in isolation and report a lack of mentoring, a lack of role models, and a grounding in self-identity that is less efficacious for their continued growth and development. As this anecdotal commentary and observation notes, often in predominantly White graduate programs with a mix of Black students who are HBCU graduates and Black graduates from predominantly White institutions, it is the HBCU graduates who appear to exert more leadership in helping establish communities of learning and identity among Black students generally that are supportive and facilitative of important support networks. A crucial question for many professors, Black and White, at predominantly White institutions who observe this phenomenon on a regular basis is, "What is so systematic about this educational strategy and alignment of actions at HBCU institutions that makes it empowering for its graduates over a lifetime of educational pursuit and attainment?"

This question of "systematic and aligned planning" is at the very core of what makes HBCU institutions so successful, resilient, productive, and mysterious, and yet so little understood from a leadership perspective. For scholars like Willie et al.(2006), the answer appears simple: "It seems that some presidents a generation ago were rising to meet contemporary challenges as indicated by their priorities" (p.23). *Ebony Towers in Higher Education: The Evolution, Mission, and Presidency of Historically Black Colleges and Universities* fills an important void in this knowledge dynamic of presidential leadership at HBCU institutions (and of the pragmatic, innovative, and ingenious leadership styles that have helped to build and support an institutional mission) that has received little attention in the research literature. The institutional mission of HBCU institutions and the forms and styles of presidential leadership that have continued to give purpose and meaning to the legacy of African American education within these institutions are critically appraised through a variety of lenses that serve to "applaud, commend, and recommend." These lenses (historical, extant research literature, legal and political, critical race commentary, and robust empirical and qualitative data) provide some of the most comprehensive views of HBCU institutions and their leadership and operational contexts to date. What is incisively clear about presidential leadership in HBCU institutions is that is it not for the "faint of heart." Because of the seamless connectivity of presidential leadership and decision making to historical purpose, institutional mission, academic and strategic planning, resource prioritization and management, and institutional development in these institutions, a new source of knowledge of leadership ingenuity and innovation is uncovered that is instructive to other collegiate leaders throughout the country "who struggle amid plates of plenty in endowment funds, gifts, and development funding." In this regard, *Ebony Towers* contributes to a greater understanding of presidential leadership style and its operational alignment at HBCU institutions in the fashion of Willie and MacLeish (1978), who debunked much of the negative portrayal of HBCU institutions by Harvard researchers Jencks and Riesman (1967) after they presented a distorted portrayal of the work of HBCU institutions and characterized them as "academic disaster areas" (p.26). The presidents chronicled in this volume are spirited about their roles of leadership; they are absolutely tenacious and utterly believable and credible in their defenses of the purposes, mission, and roles of HBCU institutions in the education of contemporary African American students and the increasing role these institutions can play in assisting other groups of students and underrepresented groups in realizing the American dream of educational opportunity.

Ultimately, *Ebony Towers* is critically significant because of the unique glimpses it provides into the leadership styles of presidents who serve as the educational and inspirational leaders of Historically Black Colleges and Universities, institutions of higher education with an unequivocal mission. Research into the qualitative nature of how these presidents operate and influence the direction and trajectory of these institutions dedicated to the education of African Americans is missing from the literature of presidential leadership in American higher education. Importantly, while HBCU institutions still educate a substantial number of African American students who seek higher education and remain faithful to their historical mission, they also are challenged by the need to: (1) further diversify their campuses in order to serve the needs and challenges of an ever increasing population and workforce; (2) foster inclusive educational communities where all voices and contributions are heard, valued, supported, and sustained in support of democratic principles; (3) foster the academic achievement and success of students through outcomes-based and experientially based programs; (4) provide dynamic, meaningful, and supportive learning environments for student retention and persistence; and (5) ground collegiate education in the needs of community service, leadership, and outreach at all levels of human interaction (governmental, corporate and non-corporate, local, state, national, and international levels) (Foster, Guyden, & Miller, 1999., p. xii). Although they share a common historical legacy of providing higher educational opportunities for African Americans and a common experience of obstacles and challenges to that mission, Historically Black Colleges and Universities are not monolithic institutions. They are public and private institutions and also find their mission in the various contexts in which they are geographically and organizationally situated—rural, urban, suburban, religiously affiliated, and/or single-sex. *Ebony Towers* illuminates the responsibilities, challenges, and opportunities of presidential leadership within this HBCU context, a highly mission-driven platform of presidential leadership and collaboration rarely known and understood by many in higher education leadership and from which much can be learned in serving a diversified population with specific and unique needs for higher education.

> Lenoar Foster
> Professor and Associate Dean for Administration,
>    Research, and Graduate Studies
> College of Education
> Washington State University

## References

Foster. L., Guyden, J. A., & Miller, A. L. (1999) (Eds.). *Affirmed action: Essays on the academic and social lives of white faculty members at historically black colleges and universities*. Lanham, MD: Rowman & Littlefield.

Jencks, C., & Riesman, D. (1967). The American Negro college. *Harvard Educational Review*, 37(1), 3–60.

United Negro College Fund (2007). Our member colleges. At: www.uncf.org (accessed December 18, 2007).

Willie, C.V., & MacLeish, M. (1978). Priorities of black college presidents. In C.V. Willie & R. Edmonds (Eds.), *Black colleges in America* (pp. 132–148). New York: Teachers College Press.

Willie, C. V., Reddick, R. J., & Brown, R. (2006). *The black college mystique.* Lanham, MD: Rowman & Littlefield.

# INTRODUCTION

The present system of American higher education reflects a history of change, growth, and development. Colleges and universities have expanded since the founding of Harvard College in 1636 to include an array of institutions (Geiger, 1999; Rudolph, 1962; Thelin, 2004; Veysey, 1965). As a result, the early purpose of educating only wealthy, White males for the ministry evolved into increased access and educational opportunity for all people in an effort to meet the changing needs of society. This transformation and expansion, however, remains the subject of much debate and criticism among educational researchers, policymakers, and the public at large. While numerous challenges arise, one of the most fundamental, critical, and recurring issues facing higher education is defining its mission (Birnbaum, 1988a; Cohen, 1998; Hartley, 2002; Stark & Lattuca, 1997; Zemsky, Wegner, & Massy, 2005).

The topic of mission is complicated further when the focus shifts to more specialized institutions of higher education. Historically Black colleges and universities (commonly referred to as HBCUs), community colleges, gender-specific institutions, and tribal colleges are different types of institutions guided by different missions intended to accommodate the needs of different student populations. The challenge, however, is, while these institutions are publicly recognized for carving their niche within the larger higher education system and serving an important function, they are often viewed with a certain level of skepticism. Perhaps the reasoning behind this skepticism lies in the public perception that traditional or mainstream higher education is the best path to guaranteed success, which makes the skeptics question the need for these *special mission* institutions. Despite the scrutiny this cohort of institutions may receive collectively, each of them has attained varying levels of success in convincing higher education stakeholders and the public at large of their value. The reality, however, is that HBCUs, more so than the other special mission institutions, disproportionately carry the burden of consistently having to justify their role in academe (Brown & Freeman, 2002; Brown, Ricard, & Donahoo, 2004; Fleming, 1984; Garibaldi,

1984). Although these institutions are recognized for their historic mission of educating a group of people previously denied an opportunity to engage in formal schooling, the current relevance of Black colleges remains an issue of contention.

The discussion concerning the need for Black colleges is particularly pressing due to the recent devastation of Hurricane Katrina. Although the hurricane damaged all colleges and universities in the state of Louisiana, only the futures of HBCUs are called into question. What is the purpose of Black colleges? Why do Black colleges continue to exist? Are Black colleges necessary? Hurricane Katrina created a safe space to allow such questions to be asked. These questions are not new; they have plagued Black colleges and universities since their inception (Allen & Jewell, 2002; Drewry & Doermann, 2001). The challenge is that it is now imperative to answer them.

According to Willie (1981b), before questions concerning the future of Black colleges can be answered, their current function must be addressed. This study examines the mission of four-year HBCUs from the perspective of the campus president to begin the process of understanding the relevance of these institutions. Presidents serve as the highest-ranking administrator within the higher education system. They maintain an all-encompassing authority and responsibility over their respective institutions, which validates their perspective on answering questions about mission.

Historically Black colleges and universities are in jeopardy (Thompson, 1998; Willie, 1994). In the *Chronicle of Higher Education*, the leading periodical on current trends and challenges affecting higher education, June (2003) identifies Black colleges as *endangered institutions*. The term *endangered*, by definition, suggests that Black colleges are on the verge of extinction. The article details the condition of Morris Brown College, a small, liberal arts historically Black college located in Atlanta, Georgia, that recently garnered national headlines due to fiscal mismanagement. The institution later lost accreditation, and the status of Morris Brown College as a viable higher education institution remains uncertain. The plight of Morris Brown College, in particular, is not an isolated incident as other Black colleges have struggled to remain open in the face of varying problems. The challenge, however, is that when problems plague one Black institution, serious implications emerge for *all* HBCUs (June, 2003).

The recent events at Morris Brown College and the devastation of Hurricane Katrina have sparked an increased interest in Black colleges across the nation. These institutions are now heavily scrutinized, and their place in the larger higher education system seems unclear. The implicit question lingers, "What purposes do HBCUs serve?" This critical question is not a new one as the root of this inquiry lies in the complex history surrounding the birth and development of these schools. Black institutions of higher education have faced blatant opposition since their inception (Allen & Jewell, 2002; Brown & Freeman, 2004; Browning & Williams, 1978; Cohen, 1998; Roebuck & Murty, 1993). Many persons in the majority population feared the notion of schooling former enslaved men, women, and their progeny, as this process would change the marginalized condition of African American people. Black colleges and universities were created as second- or third-tier institutions, as evidenced by their inadequate learning facilities, limited course offerings, less-qualified faculty, and an overall poor supply of financial resources. A stigma of inferiority continues to shadow Black colleges despite their documented progress and accomplishments over the years. The history of Black colleges shapes their current identity, and the stigma contributes to the way in which many perceive these institutions.

Morris Brown College now represents all HBCUs to both critics who condemn them and the portion of the public at large that remains unfamiliar with them. The critics view Morris Brown College as tangible evidence of the inadequacies of Black institutions. This speculation, in turn, fuels ongoing discussion concerning the overall necessity for Black colleges given their financial struggles coupled with academic opportunities available at majority-White institutions.

Benjamin E. Mays, former president of Morehouse college writes:

> No one has ever said that Catholic colleges should be abolished because they are Catholic. Nobody says that Brandeis and Albert Einstein must die because they are Jewish. Nobody says that Lutheran and Episcopalian schools should go because they are Lutheran or Episcopalian. Why should Howard University be abolished because it is known as a black university? Why pick out Negro colleges and say they must die? (1978, p. 27)

This quotation best captures the precarious condition of Black colleges and supports June's (2003) assertion that HBCUs are endangered institutions. Black colleges disproportionately have to justify their relevance within the larger higher education system, they are incessantly misunderstood, and the benefits of attending them often go unnoticed by the general public (Willie, 1994).

Fleming (1984) suggests that Black colleges' lack of adequate resources in comparison to predominantly White institutions does not solely contribute to the ongoing debate concerning the need for HBCUs. Perhaps more significant is her argument that Black colleges represent a reminder of our nation's segregated past. The existence of Black colleges challenges the American struggle toward integration, and the notion of separate schooling appears to be archaic and no longer useful or necessary.

The concept of race and understanding its implications is complex. This complexity is particularly evident in higher education where recent court decisions and changes in state and federal policies have fueled greater controversy surrounding the meaning and influence of race. According to Altbach (1991), "Race is one of the most volatile, and divisive, issues in American higher education" (p. 3). Consequently, identifying a college or university as historically Black connotes an immediate racial assumption, which is usually guided by the image of campus environments with an all-Black student population being taught by an all-Black faculty. While this is a false assumption, the immediate focus of Black colleges and universities is clearly on race, and this is what separates them from other special population institutions. Black colleges, unlike community colleges, women's colleges, men's colleges, and Hispanic-serving colleges, are racially identifiable institutions. This characteristic alone accounts for much of the disproportionate burden placed on Black colleges to substantiate their specific mission in higher education.

The consensus about the early mission of Black colleges is that they were founded for the distinct purpose of educating African American students. While this consensus describes the broad mission of these institutions, it provides little insight into the specific functions and objectives of various Black colleges and universities. Debates between W.E.B. Du Bois and Booker T. Washington heavily influenced the issue of establishing a more concrete mission of black colleges (Allen & Jewell, 2002; Brown, Donahoo, & Bertrand, 2001; Jones, 1971; Kannerstein, 1978; Willie, 1994). Washington advocated the need for vocational training and suggested that the role of Black colleges and universities is to train individuals to fill the manual labor market. Du Bois, on the other hand, argued that Black colleges should work toward building an elite group known as the "*Talented Tenth*." He believed the students should be trained to uplift the Black community by becoming professional doctors and teachers, rather than being limited to menial trades such as farming and masonry. Despite their opposing views, Washington and Du-Bois established the possibilities of Black colleges. The controversy is significant because it forced colleges to think about their responsibilities as higher education institutions.

The underlying assumption, that all HBCUs are the same, is problematic because it does not take into account the institutional differences that exist among them. Black college and university campuses vary significantly in size (two-year or four-year), sponsorship (public or private), religious affiliation, gender composition, available resources, and a host of other characteristics. Brown (2003) contends that no universal mission applies to all Black institutions. Contrary to popular opinion, HBCUs are a diverse cohort of institutions. Given the existing diversity among historically Black institutions, it is unreasonable to assume that they operate in exactly the same manner. Although these institutions are united in the historic mission of educating African Americans, each Black college and university has its own identity and set of educational objectives.

Studying college presidents is not a new phenomenon; the fascination surrounding these conspicuous figures is well documented in the academic literature (Birnbaum, 1992; Birnbaum & Umbach, 2001; Cohen & March, 1986; Fisher, 1984). Studying presidents of Black colleges, however, has been limited as presidents of these particular types of institutions are often included at the periphery of studies on college presidents at large. Although some of the responsibilities of the college presidency may be universal, studying Black college presidents requires deliberate consideration of the types of campus environments over which they preside.

Historically Black colleges and universities are among the most commented-about institutions in the academic literature, yet they remain among the least empirically examined (Brown & Freeman, 2004). A bulk of the research is heavily colloquial and anecdotal, thus leaving a void in the academic literature. Brown and Freeman (2004) suggest that, because of this absence, Black colleges continue to be described and assessed inaccurately. The available information on HBCUs traditionally falls under the guise of complimentary or controversial assertions. The complimentary research depicts Black colleges as nurturing and supportive environments and as unique institutions critical to the achievement of African American students (Allen, Epps, & Haniff, 1991; Brown, Donahoo, & Bertrand, 2001; Brown et al.,

2004; Browning & Williams, 1978; Davis, 1998; Fleming, 1984; Freeman, 1998; Garibaldi, 1984, Outcalt & Skewes-Cox, 2002). The controversial assertions, on the other hand, refer to Black colleges as academic wastelands and suggest they are cheap and inferior institutions compared to traditional or mainstream higher education (Jencks & Riesman, 1967; Wenglinsky, 1997). Despite a growing volume of research on Black colleges, different conceptions remain of what they are and what they do.

Black college research focuses primarily on two key constituents, students and faculty (Allen, 1992; Allen et al., 1991; Billingsley, 1982; Fleming, 1984, 2004; Foster, 2001; Foster & Guyden, 2004; Foster, Guyden, & Miller, 1999; Freeman, 1998; Fries-Britt, 2004; Johnson, 2001, 2004; Nettles, 1988; Slater, 1993; Thompson, 1978). This book attempts to extend the literature on HBCUs by investigating the presidents of these institutions. The president is important because he or she occupies the key position within institutions and has the power to make substantive change, particularly in terms of mission. The president regulates the institutional climate and influences the culture of the campus environment. The challenge, however, is that published research on presidents of Black colleges is virtually nonexistent. The dearth of information available on these presidents is often masked within research studies examining African American college presidents, African American administrators, or minority administrators in general (Holmes, 2004; Hoskins; 1978, Lewis, 1988). The more conventional research focuses on the experiences of African American administrators in predominantly White colleges and universities (Harvey, 1999; Jackson, 2001; Rolle, Davies, & Banning, 2000). This book is significant because it brings absolute attention to Black college campuses and the leaders of these particular institutions.

# UNDERSTANDING BLACK COLLEGES

The amended Higher Education Act of 1965 defines historically Black colleges and universities (HBCUs) as accredited institutions of higher education founded before 1964 whose primary mission was, and continues to be, the education of Black Americans (Brown, 2001; Garibaldi, 1984; Roebuck & Murty, 1993; Williams, 1988). The year 1964 is significant because it marked the passage of Title VI of the Civil Rights Act, which prohibits discrimination on the basis of race, color, or national origin within federally assisted programs and activities (Hendrickson, 1991; Williams, 1988). This book does not include predominantly Black colleges and universities, institutions of higher education with an enrollment of more than 50% African American students (Garibaldi, 1984).

The extant literature provides relevant academic research on the perceptions and perceived value attached to the nature, structure, and impact of HBCUs. Although the mission remains a relatively underdeveloped area of higher education research, the available literature on Black colleges includes a wide range of topics that help to create a holistic depiction and understanding of Black colleges and their contributions to American higher education.

## Evolution of Mission in Higher Education

In *The Ten Generations of American Higher Education*, Geiger (1999) documents the history of American institutions from the early 17th century to the present era. He identifies the period 1636 to 1740 as the Reformation Beginnings. This critically important period saw the development of the earliest North American colleges, including Harvard (1636), William and Mary

(1693), and Yale (1701). Following the pattern set by Emmanuel College (1584), now part of the University of Cambridge, church officials were highly involved with the operation of these institutions (Rudolph, 1962), and this religious presence heavily influenced the mission of the early colleges (Cohen, 1998; Veysey, 1965). Along with college matriculation, these colleges sought to train young men for the ministry (Cohen, 1998; Geiger, 1999). Duryea (1981) posits that because religious leaders during this period held dual positions in the church and government, the early institutions were responding to the public need for an educated clergy.

Although these institutions did serve a public good, the Reformation era did not provide universal access to education. Rather, education during this period was located in the Northeastern states, reserved for the upper class members of society, and designed to maintain the established class system (Jencks & Riesman, 1967; Veysey, 1965). According to Geiger (1999), students received a liberal education, focusing primarily on Aristotle's philosophies of ethics, natural science, and metaphysics. Concomitantly, the Reformation colleges valued Latin and Greek. In fact, Rudolph (1962) contends that Latin was the fundamental discipline because it was the language of the law and the church. Because knowledge in the prevailing culture tended to be expressed orally rather than in writing, institutions expected students to master a foreign language to demonstrate efficacy in communicating knowledge of the world.

Later, the birth of various colleges sparked an increase in student enrollment and a change in curricular content. The founding of the College of New Jersey in 1746 was significant because it broke the mold of the Reformation (Geiger, 1999). This institution was a provincial college and served a primarily Presbyterian population (Rudolph, 1962). Notwithstanding, the proliferation of colonial colleges (King's College, College of Philadelphia, College of Rhode Island, Queen's College, and Dartmouth) increased enrollment by accepting students of other religious denominations. Gradually a more secular approach to education emerged as a result of the development of separation of church and state during the American Revolution and establishment of the United States of America. Cohen (1998) states that, "Although they were connected with the churches, the colleges were not as much religious as educative, founded to produce a learned people" (p. 18). Colleges also began to welcome students from less prominent families, particularly the sons of farmers. While the mission of preparing clergy remained, the sons of the elite now had the opportunity to pursue law and public service (Geiger, 1999).

## Challenging the Classics

The early 19th century began with criticism of the classical college and its focus on Latin and religion. Geiger (1999) states, "Now colleges were attacked for their obsession with dead languages, for neglecting practical subjects and science, and for the continued unruliness of apparently disgruntled students" (p. 48). This dissatisfaction with the education system reflects the growing interest of students in the professions, such as law, theology, and medicine.

While some demanded that higher education systems move beyond the classical liberal education, others greatly opposed this suggested change. The Yale Report of 1828 is evidence of such opposition. Issued by Jeremiah Day and James Kingsley, it was the first unified statement of educational philosophy that focused specifically on the nature of liberal education (Conrad & Wyer, 1980). The document was a defense of the classical curriculum against the rising interest in more practical courses. According to the Report, the purpose of an undergraduate curriculum is to lay the foundation of a superior education (Conrad & Wyer, 1980; Geiger, 1999). To accomplish this goal, institutions were to furnish the mind with knowledge and create mental discipline for thinking. The curriculum, therefore, was to be limited to the classic texts, philosophy, and mathematics. The Report rejected the notion that students should specialize in particular areas of study because supporters of this philosophy believed that doing so crippled students' ability to reason, think critically, and analyze information. The Report recognized and appreciated the framework outlined by the Reformation and Colonial colleges and suggested that educational institutions return to their early mission and revitalize liberal education (Conrad & Wyer, 1980). During this era, the purpose of higher education was to indoctrinate students to value the process of learning and teach them to succeed in life, rather than to train them for the labor market.

Despite the objections of the Yale Report, higher education did become more specialized and market-influenced. Many institutions expanded their curricular offerings to add courses not included previously in the trivium and quadrivium (the classic liberal course preferred by the Yale Report). One of the strongest forces behind this curricular change was the Morrill Land-Grant Act of 1862 (Morrill Act), arguably the most important event in the curriculum shift from the general/liberal model to the utilitarian/vocational educational model (Conrad & Wyer, 1980). The Morrill Act established public institutions in every state with the support of the federal government. States did not have the resources needed to subsidize higher education, so federal government subsidies and land donations offered the best way to ensure that every state entered the realm of higher education. These institutions concentrated on providing training in industrial education, agriculture, and the mechanical arts (Geiger, 1999; Veysey, 1965). The Morrill Act is significant because it broadened the scope of educational opportunity. With these new objectives, students gained more choices, enabling them to move beyond the classical curriculum offered at most institutions.

During this time, students sought specialization. They were no longer satisfied with the liberal arts education because they wanted education to be relevant (Stark & Lattuca, 1997). Liberal education did not equip students from outside the upper classes with the tools necessary to gain employment. The increasing interest in specialized education grew out of students' desire to receive training in a particular profession to acquire a specific skill (Conrad & Wyer, 1980). In this era, practical education gained greater influence over the mission of higher education.

### Broadening Access

Although the curriculum was changing, higher education remained primarily the province of White males until after the Civil War (Cohen, 1998; Thelin, 2004). Following the war, the demise of slavery promoted other social revisions and reforms, including attacks on the kind of educational exclusion that was prevalent. Women and minorities used this time to fight for educational access and equal rights. Responding to these new demands, higher education took action. Although equalizing educational opportunity occurred gradually, colleges and universities began to open admissions to both women and minorities during the mid-19th century.

In 1837, Oberlin College became the first institution to admit women (Cohen, 1998; Rudolph, 1962; Thelin, 2004). Later, between 1861 and 1875, Matthew Vassar, Henry Wells, Sophia Smith, and Henry Durant created colleges exclusively for women (Geiger, 1999). These institutions allowed women to participate fully in higher education at institutions where they were the focus of both the curriculum and the administration. While the mission of these colleges catered to the needs of women, their purpose was to educate them to succeed at the tasks assigned to them in an industrializing society, especially rearing educated children (Geiger, 1999).

People of color also gained greater access to higher education during the 19th century to prepare them to take their designated place in the social order. In addition to omitting women, the American system of higher education initially failed to address the educational needs of minorities, particularly African Americans (Brown, Donahoo, & Bertrand, 2001; Davis, 1998; Fleming, 1984; Thompson, 1998). With few exceptions, slavery precluded widespread interest in educating people of African decent (Brown, 1999; Brown & Hendrickson, 1997; Lindsay, 1998). Indeed, plantation owners' strong resistance to even the suggestion that slavery might end made it illegal to teach bondsmen and bondswomen how to read or write. As a result, most freedmen and freedwomen left slavery lacking the most basic literacy skills (Foner, 1988; Roebuck & Murty, 1993). Indeed, slavery by itself did not prevent African Americans from accessing schools; few Black people gained access to formal educational opportunities before the Civil War, regardless of their legal status (Brown & Hendrickson, 1997).

Social reforms such as expanding higher education access to women and minorities led to additional changes in the curriculum of various institutions. Geiger (1999) designates the period from 1850 to 1890 as the New Departures generation. During this time, American higher education absorbed the Germanic ideals of *lehrfreiheit* (freedom to teach) and *lernfreiheit* (freedom to learn) with the opening of Johns Hopkins University in 1876 (Conrad & Wyer, 1980). This system of education, which focused primarily on research and science, gave birth to what Geiger (2000) calls the multipurpose college. Unlike the institutional structures before it, the multipurpose college promoted many missions simultaneously. Rather than concentrate on either classical courses or vocational training, the multipurpose college offered both, affording students the opportunity to explore various academic areas.

Around the time the multipurpose college developed, another type of higher education institution also arose. The availability of two-year, or community, colleges increased enrollment in and access to higher education (Geiger, 2000). Formerly known as junior colleges, these institutions developed before 1910, but grew rapidly after 1940 (Stark & Lattuca, 1997). Geiger

(1999) declares that these colleges had a profound impact on higher education by expanding the market for a college education to people who might want to learn new things, but are not necessarily able to complete, or interested in completing, a four-year degree. Community colleges developed to provide vocational instruction and initially act as stepping-stones to four-year institutions. These colleges increased higher education access because they enrolled a significant number of local poor, working-class, and minority students. The overall mission of these colleges was and often continues to be to train individuals for the workforce. The community college enables people from less privileged backgrounds to participate in higher education without traveling far from home, enduring economic hardships, or committing to an academic program that takes years to complete.

Similar to that of the multipurpose college, the curriculum at the community colleges has been and remains quite diverse. Although community colleges often focus on vocational training, their local nature also allows them to offer enrichment courses for members of the community at large. In doing so, community colleges expanded higher education opportunity by encouraging people of all ages, cultures, and social backgrounds to become lifelong learners. The Servicemen's Readjustment Act of 1944, commonly referred to as the GI Bill of Rights, also played a significant role in expanding the higher education landscape (Cohen, 1998). President Franklin D. Roosevelt signed the bill, which provided returning World War II veterans with the opportunity to acquire a college education with assistance from the federal government.

### The Curriculum

While much more diverse than the classical education championed by the Yale Report, curriculum remains a hotly contested area. Higher education in the 19th century showcased a battle between classical and vocational training spurred on by the Yale Report. Although the Morrill Act supported and perpetuated practical training, the 20th century witnessed the pendulum swinging back toward the model of general education as evidenced in Harvard's distribution of *General Education in a Free Society* (also known as the *Harvard Redbook*) in 1945 (Stark & Lattuca, 1997). Although this document supported preserving general education, it acknowledged that specializing in a particular field of study was also valuable due to the changing nature of the world.

The contention expressed by the *Harvard Redbook* remains to this day, and diverse and often contradictory views about the mission of higher education remain an important matter of discussion. One of the most popular debates during the 20th century concerning the mission of higher education occurred between John Dewey and Robert Maynard Hutchins. Commonly referred to as the debate of general versus specialized education, the conflict between Dewey and Hutchins extended the controversy started by the Yale Report years earlier. Ehrlich (1997) details the contents of this argument; however, the key issue was the nature and purpose of a liberal education.

In determining the nature of a liberal education, Hutchins promoted the view that each individual should control his or her own learning. Arguing in favor of a more natural and classical view of education, Hutchins proposed a moratorium approach to learning and thinking. He believed that students should be detached from the consequences of the real world and spared the practicality of life during their time in school. In his view, liberal education should provide students with absolute truths and ideals found only in the great books of Western civilization. The goal, therefore, was intellectual inquiry, gaining knowledge for the sake of higher learning. Hutchins argues that the problem with higher education was that it had attached a service-station concept to the university: because society makes demands on colleges and universities, systems of higher education should respond to them. For Hutchins, this pressure on institutions to become more specialized was problematic because it lessened the value of attending college and interfered with giving students a true liberal arts education (Ehrlich, 1997).

On the other side of this debate, Dewey suggested that the goal of education was to make democracy work. In his opinion, education should move beyond satisfying the personal gratification of students and the task of preparing them for specific professions. Contrary to Hutchins's perspective, Dewey rejected the notion of implanting fixed truths into the minds of students because he believed that they crippled a student's ability to formulate ideas and think critically. Dewey believed that students learn best by working together and experiencing the world, and he warned the system of higher education against dividing intellect and experience. In his opinion, the key to a successful liberal education was in merging the two (Ehrlich, 1997).

## Birth and Development of Historically Black Colleges and Universities

Similar to other long-standing issues in higher education, the nature and purpose of Black colleges receive regular reconsideration. Research indicates that, to understand and appreciate the complexity surrounding Black colleges, it is imperative to acknowledge their historic roots and evolution (Brown, 1999; Brown, Donahoo, & Bertrand, 2001; Browning & Williams, 1978; Davis, 1998; Drewry & Doermann, 2001; Roebuck & Murty, 1993). As previously indicated, the U.S. system of higher education did not provide universal collegiate access. In fact, early institutions such as Harvard and Yale tended to deny access to individuals who were not wealthy, Protestant, male, and White (Brown, Donahoo, & Bertrand, 2001). Before the American Civil War, the combination of slavery and segregation restricted educational access and opportunity for Black Americans. With few exceptions, Black students were summarily denied entry to institutions of higher learning. During this time, most African Americans lived in the South, where laws prohibited enslaved men, women, and children from learning the fundamentals of reading and writing. In an attempt to make education more accessible, the American Missionary Association (AMA) began the movement to develop systems of schooling that indoctrinated and educated former enslaved individuals and their progeny (Browning & Williams, 1978). This system of schooling began as primary and secondary schools and later evolved into collegiate-level education, thus giving birth to HBCUs.

Following the lead of the AMA, historically Black colleges were funded and established by Black churches, the Freedman's Bureau, local communities, and private philanthropists (Brown, 1999). The growth of these institutions persisted during a tumultuous time in American history. Roebuck & Murty (1993) assert: "They were founded and developed in an environment unlike that surrounding other colleges—that is, in a hostile environment marked by legal segregation and isolation from mainstream United States higher education. Historically they have served a population that has lived under severe legal, educational, economic, political, and social restrictions" (p. 3). Roebuck and Murty clearly indicate that the historical context in which these institutions developed is critical to understanding their function in the larger higher education landscape, particularly as it relates to African Americans.

Since Black colleges formed outside the traditional system of learning and catered to a population of people who were perpetually denied access to education, the early objectives of these institutions focused on uplifting the condition of the Black community (Davis, 1998). According to Walters (1991), the goals of Black colleges include: (a) maintenance of Black historical and cultural tradition; (b) provision of key leadership in the Black community; (c) development of economic stability in the Black community; (d) presentation of Black role models who are able to interpret the way in which political, social, or economic dynamics impact the Black community; (e) production of college graduates equipped with the competence to deal with problems arising between minority and majority populations; and (f) ability to produce Black agents for specialized research, training, and information dissemination. The goals identify the expectations of HBCUs; the expectations, in turn, mandate responsibilities that Black colleges assume.

Similarly, Jones (1971) contends that HBCUs have an inherent responsibility to uplift the overall condition of Black people and strengthen the communities in which they live. Black colleges must open their doors and teach and help those who may not be fortunate enough to be registered students. Jones (1971), however, identifies White oppression as the major obstacle that prevents Black colleges and universities from carrying out their duties successfully. Racist ideologies interfere with the prosperity of HBCUs due to the desire to preserve these schools as subordinate pieces in the larger higher education puzzle.

## The Debate: Booker T. Washington Versus W.E.B. Du Bois

Since their inception, HBCUs have assumed a dual responsibility with regard to positioning and preparing their students for future success. Black colleges must meet the same curriculum standards as predominantly White institutions while simultaneously offering African Americans an education that is culturally relevant. Benjamin E. Mays (1978) advised, "They must be as much concerned with Shakespeare, Tennyson, and Marlowe as the white colleges. But the Negro institutions must give equal emphasis to the writings of Paul Dunbar, Countee Cullen, and Langston Hughes" (p. 28). This challenge imposed on Black colleges contributed to the discourse concerning these institutions' curriculum plans.

The most popular debate occurred between Booker T. Washington and W.E.B. Du Bois (Allen & Jewell, 2002; Brown, Donahoo, & Bertrand, 2001; Fleming, 1984; Jones, 1971; Kannerstein, 1978; Willie, 1994), who held opposing views with respect to the nature of Black education. Although viewed as adversaries, the two men debated publicly as a political strategy to bring attention to HBCUs. Washington advocated for vocational training and suggested that the role of Black colleges and universities was to train individuals to fill the manual labor market. Du Bois, on the other hand, argued that Black colleges should work toward building an elite group commonly described as the *Talented Tenth*. He believed that students should be trained to uplift the Black community by becoming doctors and teachers, rather than being limited to trades such as farming and masonry. The controversy helped Black colleges find value in including both perspectives by creating learning environments that offered students industrial *and* liberal arts courses.

## The Issue of Desegregation

The educational haven provided by Black colleges does not preclude the fact that these institutions began as instruments of racial segregation. Due to the long history of racial inequalities, "states created dual collegiate structures of public education, most of which operated exclusively for whites in one system and African Americans in the other" (Brown & Hendrickson, 1997, p. 96). According to Patterson (1994), the current racial identifiability of the South's dual system reflects the creation and existence of the institutions as segregated entities. The dual system continues, despite desegregation decisions rendered by the Supreme Court.

There has been a lack of consensus on the policy, legislation, and judicial remedy needed to overcome the continuing effects of segregation in higher education institutions. There is a lack of clarity regarding the definition of desegregation and the criteria for compliance. Higher education is still without "a prevailing legal standard that clearly articulates what it means for postsecondary education to be desegregated or to have dismantled dual educational structures" (Brown, 1999, p. xviii). As a result of this confusion, desegregation remains a concern for public Black colleges and universities as they are often the primary targets of desegregation initiatives.

Through a series of important court cases, African Americans have consistently challenged racial policies and pursued full implementation of equal status. In 1896, the U.S. Supreme Court ruled, in *Plessy v. Ferguson*, that segregation of races was constitutional as long as the facilities and conditions for Blacks were equal in quality to those provided for Whites (Johnson, 1993), a principle that became known as "separate but equal." As a result, revised state constitutions and state laws prohibited Black and White students from attending the same schools (Roebuck & Murty, 1993). Consequently, in 1954, *Brown v. Board of Education* ruled that separating students solely based on race was unconstitutional, so separate educational facilities were essentially unequal (Cohen, 1998). Johnson (1993) contends, "The decision was in response to the deplorable conditions in which African Americans were educated and forced to live—conditions that were the result of legally sanctioned segregation" (p.140). *Brown* focused on desegregation in primary and secondary public education; the thrust to dismantle dual systems was not extended to higher education until passage of Title VI of the Civil Rights Act of 1964 (Brown, 1999). With the passage of Title VI, states supporting dual systems of higher education were required by law to dismantle them (Thompson, 1998).

Despite federal law's mandate to eliminate all systems of segregation, 19 states (notably in the South) continued to operate dual systems: Alabama, Arkansas, Delaware, Florida, Georgia, Kentucky, Louisiana, Maryland, Mississippi, Missouri, North Carolina, Ohio, Oklahoma, Pennsylvania, South Carolina, Tennessee, Texas, Virginia, and West Virginia (Brown, 1999). This system only affirmed inequality and enforced the practice of discrimination. The problem was that "the law did not identify what was meant by discrimination based on race or national origin—it just outlawed it. The meaning of discrimination, desegregation, and compliance were not even explored in the legislative evolution of Title VI" (Brown, 1999, p. 8). Therefore, states had the autonomy to interpret the law to meet their particular needs. This inevitably allowed states to uphold the segregated system of higher education.

## United States v. Fordice

The highly publicized case of *United States v. Fordice* found that the state of Mississippi was operating segregated schools. In 1975, private plaintiff Jake

Ayers, along with the United States, filed a lawsuit against the state of Mississippi, contending that de jure (by law) segregation still existed in higher education. The complaint alleged that HBCUs remained separate and inferior to White institutions due to discriminatory practices in student admissions, employment of faculty and staff, mission designations, and funding (Patterson, 1994). The trial court (1987) and the Fifth Circuit Court of Appeals (1990) ruled in favor of Mississippi, finding that the state had fulfilled its duty to dismantle its earlier system by adopting and implementing racially neutral policies and procedures for all students to attend the institutions of their choice. The plaintiff appealed to the Supreme Court.

On June 26, 1992, the U.S. Supreme Court reversed and remanded the ruling of the Court of Appeals, declaring that Mississippi had not desegregated its dual system of higher education. The Court also stated that the legal standard applied in the lower level was incorrect, that is, although the state university system appeared to be unbiased, noticeable factors governed an individual's choice of institution, particularly if that individual were an African American. The Court went on to say that Mississippi's eight public institutions remained racially identifiable; therefore, the principal requirement of the state was to eradicate all remnants and vestiges of de jure segregation which were not "educationally justifiable" and could be "practically eliminated" (Brown & Hendrickson, 1997).

According to Brown (1995), *United States v. Fordice* "outlined the financial implications for public historically black colleges and universities in American higher education systems" (p. 35). The case exposed the funding discrepancies and showed just how separate and unequal HBCUs remained. Rather than integrating the campuses or increasing funds for predominantly Black universities, Mississippi proposed closing some of the Black schools and merging them with stronger and better-funded institutions which are almost exclusively White. Many believe the *Fordice* litigation could ring the death knell of public Black colleges in the South (Cross & Slater, 1995, p. 79).

Brown (1999) argues that the success of collegiate desegregation is contingent upon the willingness of higher education to "(a) redesignate the missions and institutional statements of those institutions designed to deliver inferior service, (b) redefine the financial formula whereby institutions are funded, (c) reassess the standards of institutional admission, and (d) reinterpret the possibility of incongruent collegiate populations" (p. 11). The problem, however, is that when desegregation plans are initiated, Black colleges and universities are targeted. Just as in the case of *Fordice*, the desegregation decision threatened the closure and merger of Black institutions, not predominantly White colleges and universities. Yet unfinished, collegiate desegregation remains a critically important issue with regard to Black college research.

## The Mission of Historically Black Colleges and Universities

Similar to desegregation, mission issues continue to affect the perception of HBCUs. Indeed, the topic of mission remains a relatively unexplored area of current Black college research. In 1978, Kannerstein conducted a research study focusing specifically on the topic of mission, *Black Colleges: Self Concept.* In investigating the purpose, aims, and overall objectives of HBCUs by analyzing newsletters, catalogues, and other official publications from a select sample of schools, Kannerstein sought to understand how Black colleges perceive themselves based on the information they provide to others. He argued that this information represents their identity and role within the larger system of higher education and, ultimately, communicates these schools' self-concepts. Although Kannerstein (1978) neglects to describe the details of the research method, he does reveal that most of the information was taken from Harvard University's Center for Urban Studies' collection of various school publications. He examined numerous publications from different HBCUs in addition to some predominantly White colleges and university publications for comparative purposes. The information revealed provides insights about HBCUs' missions and initiates a discussion of why Black colleges are important.

In studying mission, Kannerstein (1978) identified the following eight themes that Black colleges deem critical to fulfill their mission: (a) community service, (b) open enrollment, (c) democracy, citizenship, and leadership, (d) social change, (e) concern about health, (f) ethics and values, (g) educational emphases, and (h) Black studies. These findings represent the select sample of schools and may not be indicative of all HBCUs because the researcher does not provide an exact account of how many schools he investigated.

### *Community Service*

Based on Kannerstein's (1978) study, Black colleges stress the importance of community service and do not view it as peripheral to teaching and research responsibilities. Civic engagement, commitment to the community, and public service are invaluable components of Black college life and are ingrained into the mission of these institutions, as evidenced in their curriculum, research initiatives, and teaching instruction (Kannerstein, 1978). Defining community service is complex, however; for the purpose of this study, it includes ideals such as promoting racial understanding, providing financial aid to students in need, developing educational programs for adults, and acknowledging and responding to the needs of the Black community and the world at large.

Kannerstein (1978) highlights a few examples of how Black colleges incorporate community service into the fabric of their schools, and this tangible evidence helps to promote a clearer understanding of various institutions' priorities. Kentucky State University, for example, encourages students to contribute the cultural and economic growth of the community; Miles College incorporates special programs such as Upward Bound and Head Start; Langston University proposes that students help in solving problems plaguing the state of Oklahoma; Spelman College promotes the importance of social involvement and political activism; and Howard University focuses on improving the District of Columbia and eliminating the conditions that affect African American people negatively. According to Kannerstein (1978), the dedication of HBCUs toward inculcating community service into their institutional missions is perhaps their greatest contribution to the American higher education system, and other colleges and universities should embrace and emulate these institutions' commitment to service.

## *Open Enrollment*

Despite HBCUs' commitment to community service, one of the biggest challenges they face is the misconception that they are reserved for African Americans. Kannerstein (1978) calls attention to the fact Black institutions of higher education have an open enrollment policy, which suggests that these institutions embrace all individuals, irrespective of race, gender, national origin, and other identifiable attributes. Xavier University of Louisiana, for example, is the only historically Black Catholic institution in the country, and many of its students are non-Catholic and White. Lincoln University (Pennsylvania), Dillard University, Fisk University, and Paine College promote the importance of diverse campus environments by clearly articulating this philosophy throughout their official school publications. The idea of diversification at Black colleges is not limited to the student body, but extends as well to faculty, staff, and administration (Foster & Guyden, 2004). The misconception is that Black colleges only benefit African Americans. The open enrollment philosophy is not new to Black colleges, nor was this notion imposed on them by legal authority. Historically Black colleges and universities were founded on the premise that everyone deserves an opportunity to pursue higher education. According to Kannerstein (1978), "the concern of black colleges is not with who gets in but what happens to them afterward" (p. 37). Their focus is on helping students, regardless of their background and disadvantaged circumstances, to become productive and successful citizens.

### *Democracy, Citizenship, and Leadership*

Historically Black colleges and universities stress the importance of equipping their graduates with the tools necessary to make meaningful contributions to society. Kannerstein (1978) found throughout nearly every publication he examined an emphasis on viewing education as a democracy. He learned that Black colleges encouraged students to engage in civic participation and promoted the value of leadership. The mission statement for Southern University, for example, specifically proclaims that its goal is to instill students with a sense of responsibility to carry out the duties of citizenship. In addition, a primary objective of Spelman College is to prepare African American women for leadership positions, and Livingstone College promotes students to be conscious and aware and condemns acts of snobbery and distinctions based on class or socioeconomic status.

### *Social Change*

In addition to preparing their students for leadership in a democratic society, the need for change is a common priority among Black colleges and universities. Their mission is for students to recognize the condition of the world, particularly that of the African American community, and strive toward improvement and growth. According to Kannerstein (1978) the catalogues of Black colleges and predominantly White colleges differ in terms of how they depict their view of the world. Historically Black colleges and universities highlight the constant struggles and inequalities that plague society, whereas predominantly White schools portray a picture of peace and equal opportunity. Students enrolled at Black colleges, therefore, receive added inspiration to work for change because they realize the world often discriminates against them just because of the color of their skin. The responsibility of Black colleges is to provide students with the vocational tools to prepare them to meet the demands of today's changing society. Tougaloo College emphasizes the need for students to be familiar with new technology and advancement, and Clark College (now Clark Atlanta University) proposes that students be professionally prepared to address the challenges posed by the present and the problems of the future.

## Concern About Health

For HBCUs, professionalism and community uplift also include attention to physical health and wellness. Health is a general concern for all people, particularly college students. African American students, however, are at a considerable disadvantage because some of them have had less exposure to health education and proper medical care prior to attending college. Kannerstein (1978) suggests that, to remedy the situation, Black colleges have assumed the role of in loco parentis (in place of the parent) and broadened their mission to include health matters. The publications analyzed for the study reveal that the concept of health extends beyond the mere act of physical activity. Grambling College (now Grambling State University), University of Arkansas at Pine Bluff, and Oakwood College emphasize the importance of balancing physical, mental, and spiritual health. Black colleges tend to focus on students in their totality.

## Ethics and Values

As part of their attention to educating students in mind, body, and spirit, HBCUs play a key role in influencing student development and growth outside the confines of the classroom. The apparent mission of these colleges and universities extends beyond academic preparation to include responsibility for producing graduates who possess character and good judgment. Kannerstein (1978) declares that Black colleges display greater emphasis on ethics and values than do predominantly White institutions based on the information found in the official school publications. Barber-Scotia College encourages students to take responsibility for their actions, acquire integrity, and respect individual differences, and Tougaloo College concentrates on equipping students with a sense of generosity, tolerance, and acceptance. Because many private HBCUs are affiliated with churches, numerous mission statements mention the need to maintain a healthy spiritual connection. Rust

College advances that Christian values are an integral part of its institution's fabric and are critical to student development.

## Educational Emphases

Even with their efforts to develop the whole student, Black colleges have never neglected or ignored the academic portion of their mission. Early on, W.E.B. Du Bois and Booker T. Washington debated the purpose of education for African American people. Du Bois believed that the focus should be on the liberal arts, while Washington advocated for more vocational preparation. The findings of Kannerstein's (1978) research study suggest that HBCUs have successfully combined the two perspectives by recognizing that both educational objectives are necessary for college students. Historically Black institutions of higher education value liberal arts education and vocational training and promote this concept throughout their catalogues and bulletin announcements. LeMoyne-Owen College, Fisk University, and Lincoln University (Pennsylvania) offer students the opportunity to pursue the humanities, social sciences, and fine arts, while also preparing them for their careers in such fields such as engineering, business, and architecture.

## Black Studies

In addition to the liberal and vocational educational programs offered at Black colleges, these institutions perform the added service of creating a curriculum in American history and cultural studies that includes the accomplishments of African Americans. The promotion of Black studies at HBCUs reflects the recognition that the African American experience is an integral part of American history. The idea of Black studies is not limited to a few course offerings that students take as elective requirements. Rather, Black colleges create learning environments in which African American history and culture are appreciated and celebrated, and they advertise this unapologetically in their official school publications (Kannerstein, 1978). Xavier University of Louisiana boasts that, although the institution serves the community at large, its priorities lie with issues related to African American people. In addition, Morehouse College attempts to prepare graduates to perform well in their professional careers while also maintaining a commitment to the Black community, and Stillman College says, "knowledge and understanding of the history and culture of black and other peoples and how they have interrelated through the years are essential to the promulgation of truth" (Kannerstein, 1978, p. 48).

These eight themes discovered by Kannerstein (1978) provide a glimpse into what HBCUs value as necessary tools to fulfill their mission. The study is helpful because it initiates discussion of the mission of Black schools, a topic that educational researchers often overlook. As a result, the study serves as a starting point for future research. School catalogues, bulletins, alumni newsletters, and other publications are formal documentation that all institutions of higher education produce. Who is responsible for communicating this information, and where does it come from? The next logical step in terms of research is to attempt to connect what is written on paper and what actually happens on Black college campuses. The means to attain this information lies in seeking out individuals directly involved with these campuses to get a more in-depth perspective on the mission of Black colleges and universities.

# BLACK CAMPUS POPULATIONS

Although research on Black colleges remains limited, much of the information available focuses on students who attend these institutions. Research studies on students at historically Black colleges and universities (HBCUs) include an array of topics ranging from issues pertaining to college choice to comparisons between the learning environments at Black colleges and predominantly White institutions. Educators are concerned with the overall experience of students while attending these institutions. The researchers recognize that the college or university a student attends is an important determinant of educational satisfaction, professional development, and future success. Black colleges serve a specific purpose, and studying their students provides an opportunity to learn about the impact of these institutions—both their contributions and challenges within the higher education landscape. As Fleming (1984) indicates, students at Black colleges rely heavily on and establish strong relationships with their faculty members. Indeed, faculty members employed at Black colleges assume enormous responsibility. Since Black colleges were created as an intentional subordinate tier of traditional higher education (Brown, Ricard, & Donahoo, 2004), faculty must work hard to provide the students of such a system with the necessary tools to function and prosper in society.

## Students at Historically Black Colleges and Universities

Given their ability to enroll in any institution type, many question why some students continue to choose to attend Black colleges and universities. McDonough, Antonio, and Trent (1997) examined factors that affect the college choice decision-making processes of African American students. More specifically, they wanted to find out if students who choose predominantly

White institutions have different college choice processes from those who select HBCUs. The researchers used data collected as part of the Cooperative Institutional Research Program's 1993 freshman survey, which included questions about students' background and demographics, experiences in high school, reasons for going to college, reasons for choosing their particular institution, and expectations about college.

The study revealed the following Black college predictors: (a) religious affiliation of college; (b) good social reputation; (c) desire to become more cultured; (d) relatives' wishes; (e) a friend's suggestion; (f) parents' wishes; and (g) ability of graduates to secure employment. Students provided the following reasons for attending predominantly White institutions: (a) recruitment by athletic department; (b) desire to live near home; (c) good academic reputation; (d) availability of financial aid; (e) advice of high school counselor; and (f) particular educational programs. In analyzing the differences, the researchers found that students at Black colleges demonstrated higher rates of attaining a bachelor's degree than at predominantly White colleges, greater gains in academic achievement, better social integration, and higher occupational aspirations.

Likewise, Freeman (1999) conducted a qualitative longitudinal study focused on understanding the characteristics of students in regard to the college choice process. The sample consisted of 21 students identified as high achieving. All of the students attended predominantly Black high schools and were reared in predominantly Black neighborhoods. The findings showed that the characteristics of the students were similar, regardless of their choice to attend an HBCU or a predominantly White institution. All of the students cited financial aid as a major consideration in their decision. While the lack of financial aid is particularly problematic for HBCUs, these findings demonstrate that Black colleges are improving their ability to attract high achieving students.

## College Impact

The decision to attend an HBCU or a predominantly White school is subjective, and numerous factors contribute to the choices students make, as evidenced in the studies conducted by McDonough, Antonio, and Trent (1997) and Freeman (1999). Those researchers explored the reasoning behind students' choices, the *why* factor. The next logical step is understanding the *how* factor: How does the choice of attending an HBCU or a predominantly White institution affect the college experience of African American students? Fleming (1984) explores this topic in a study revered as a major contribution to the field of higher education. Her heavily cited book, *Blacks in College: A Comparative Study of Students' Success in Black and in White Institutions*, focuses on the contributions these schools make to African Americans. Fleming (1984) tests the common assumptions about the impact of Black colleges. Are predominantly White schools better for African American students because they have more resources? Do historically Black schools provide a more supportive learning environment? Are African Americans students isolated on predominantly White campuses? Are Black students progressing academically at a higher rate when enrolled in an HBCU?

A trained psychologist, Fleming (1984) concentrates on understanding mental processes and behaviors, so she is primarily concerned with the students and how they internalize their experiences rather than the higher education institutions per se. The schools, which serve as the backdrop to the study, provide a setting for comparison for the researcher to understand what happens to African American students enrolled in Black colleges versus predominantly White schools. Most comparative studies on Black and White higher education institutions yield information that cannot be compared because researchers ask different questions depending on the learning environment (Fleming, 1984). The strength of this research, particularly as it relates to HBCUs, lies in the method. Studies pertaining to Black colleges are often not empirically based. This cross-sectional study, however, consisted of approximately 3,000 freshman and senior students (both Black and White) enrolled in 15 colleges throughout Ohio, Georgia, Texas, and Mississippi. The sample of institutions included eight predominantly White schools and seven predominantly Black schools. The collection of data spanned three years, and all students endured the same rigorous testing for approximately four to eight hours. They participated in personal interviews, completed questionnaires, and submitted their transcripts for evaluation. Additionally, the students engaged in tests of cognitive growth.

The research findings do not hide the negative truths often associated with HBCUs. According to Fleming (1984), "They only suggest that their deleterious impact on intellectual development is overestimated and that the significance of opportunities for academic progress, social participation, and interpersonal belonging is underestimated" (p. 150). Students overwhelming reported poor teacher quality, yet they boasted about the positive relationships they developed with their professors. The students valued the informal mentoring and words of encouragement from their professors on Black college campuses. Although HBCUs lack adequate resources, they do provide a more supportive and nurturing environment than do predominantly White campuses. A supportive environment does not equate to a place of complete perfection and harmony, as evidenced by students on Black college campuses' positive *and* negative experiences.

Based on the data provided by participants, Fleming (1984) identifies three key aspects of a supportive learning environment. First, students must have the opportunity to connect with other people. On Black college campuses, students are better able to build relationships with their peers, in addition to faculty and staff who can serve as role models. Second, students should be able to get involved with campus life. Historically Black colleges and universities offer more opportunities for students to participate in extracurricular activities, particularly leadership roles. African American students on predominantly White campuses often feel a sense of powerlessness and are unable to engage fully in the college experience. Third, a supportive environment must provide a space where students feel able to succeed academically. Black college faculties are more likely to take the time to help students and affirm that they are capable of achieving. Students report that faculty at predominantly White institutions lack interest in their well-being and development. Overall, Fleming's (1984) research does not advocate that Black students should abandon predominantly White colleges and universities. These findings simply reveal students' experiences so that and both historically Black and predominantly White institutions of higher education are able to use this information to improve their learning environments and better serve their students.

## Faculty at Historically Black Colleges and Universities

Despite the rich history concerning the evolution and challenges of HBCUs, little is known about the faculty at these institutions. Few empirical studies focus on the experiences of this particular cohort of educators (Johnson, 2004). In one of the few studies examining faculty work at Black colleges, Roebuck and Murty (1993) provide information regarding the racial composition of faculty at HBCUs. In their studies on identifying the role of Black institutions, they report that approximately 55% of Black college faculties are African American, 40% are White Americans, and other non-Black minorities comprise the remaining 5% of the total faculty composition at HBCUs. The diversity of the faculty at Black colleges is not similar on predominantly White campuses; in fact, African American faculty are highly underrepresented at majority-White institutions (Turner & Myers, 2000). Moore and Wagstaff (1974) propose that Black educators prefer Black campuses because of their concern for educating Black students. The professors feel a sense of obligation to give back to their communities. Furthermore, most HBCUs value teaching and service, and African American professors often favor this approach as opposed to the research focus on most predominantly White campuses. However, the challenges that concern faculty at Black colleges include low salaries, meager institutional resources, and lack of respect with regard to professional recognition (Diener, 1985; Thompson, 1978).

Expanding on earlier studies, current research on faculty at HBCUs centers on the socialization process (Johnson, 2004) and the increased presence of White faculty members (Foster & Guyden, 2004). Johnson (2004) asserts that Black colleges must be proactive about implementing policies and procedures ensuring that faculty members engage in a positive and effective socialization process. The researcher suggests, for example, developing orientation programs that would aid faculty in building commitment and loyalty to the institution while allowing them time to get to know their colleagues. Monthly orientation meetings would provide a means for the institution to stay in contact with the faculty and assist them with any problems or other pertinent matters. The overall goal of the socialization process is to increase the retention of faculty at Black colleges.

Examining socialization in conjunction with racial issues, Foster and Guyden (2004) concentrate on White faculty and their experiences on Black college campuses. The founding of Black colleges rests partially on the shoulders of White missionaries; therefore, their presence on the faculty is not a new phenomenon. The researchers indicate that some White faculty are drawn to HBCUs because of a personal commitment to diversity, while others are recruited as a result of desegregation initiatives at Black institutions.

## Diversity on the Historically Black College Campus

The race of faculty members is just one of the ways that diversity affects the modern Black college. Beyond the limited scope of race, diversity in higher education includes a variety of concerns that influence the mission and students of each institution. Colleges and universities are identified in myriad ways. Terms such as community college, liberal arts, research intensive, and doctoral granting provide a clear indication of the focus of the institutions and what they offer. The term, historically Black, however, shifts the focus from *what* is being offered to *whom* it is being offered to. "Historically Black" connotes assumptions about colleges and universities based on race first. The assumption persists that these particular schools are reserved for African American students, administrators, and faculty. The reality remains that, while most HBCUs are predominantly Black in population, they are not exclusively Black. A growing body of research focusing on the experiences of White students and faculty suggests that access and opportunity provided by HBCUs are not limited to people of African decent.

Building on the work initiated by Fleming (1984), Conrad, Brier, and Braxton (1997) conducted a thorough examination of the experiences of White students enrolled in HBCUs. The researchers used an open-ended, multiple case study design and conducted individual interviews and focus groups with students, faculty, and administrators on historically Black college campuses. The study included the following five public institutions of higher education: North Carolina Agricultural and Technical State University, Winston-Salem University, Southern University at New Orleans, Kentucky State University, and Savannah State College. The researchers purposely selected these Black colleges and universities because of their success in attracting a significant number of White students and because some of the schools received court mandates to desegregate.

The interviews Conrad et al. (1997) conducted focused on one key question: What important factors contribute to White students' attendance at HBCUs? Initially, the researchers asked participants to share their experiences and elaborate on this question. However, after two on-campus visits, the researchers developed a rating instrument based on the information gathered through the initial interviews. Conrad et al. (1997) identified 14 major factors that influence the increased presence of White students on Black college and university campuses and grouped them into three categories: (a) academic program offerings, (b) student financial support, and (c) institutional characteristics. It is important to note that the five participating institutions, like most HBCUs, are located in close proximity to predominantly White colleges and universities, and some participants' responses reflect the implications of this situation. In their analysis, Conrad et al. (1997) divided the data into three categories: academic program offerings, student financial support, and institutional characteristics.

## Academic Program Offerings

Conrad et al. (1997) ranked the following responses in terms of importance to students: (a) program offerings in high-demand fields of study; (b) unique program offerings; (c) alternative program delivery systems; (d) graduate program offerings; and (e) positive reputation for quality. The participants reported that Black colleges offered quality academic programs, particularly in demanding and competitive fields such as nursing, business, and engineering. One student said the engineering program was so strong at North Carolina A&T that he could "overlook that it's a black school" (Conrad et al., p. 43). This short statement speaks volumes in regard to the negative perception often associated with Black colleges and universities. The researchers discovered that HBCUs attracted White students because they offered unique programs not available at predominantly White institutions. Students enrolled in more specialized fields of study and were able to pursue disciplines outside of mainstream academia. The students revealed that many of the White institutions imposed enrollment caps limiting the number of students allowed to pursue a specific academic major, so they opted to attend the historically Black institution.

In addition to academic offerings, many of the students favored HBCUs because of their varied campus delivery systems. The Black schools offered more flexibility in terms of weekend and evening course offerings, which appealed to nontraditional students such as part-time students and adult learners. The convenience of the program offerings afforded them the opportunity to fulfill other obligations, particularly with regard to work and family. The interviewees valued the graduate programs, specifically at the master's level, that HBCUs offered. The programs equipped students with a competitive edge and contributed to their overall marketability in the job market. According to Conrad et al. (1997), study participants readily admitted the importance of the school's reputation. Although they enrolled in institutions identified as historically Black, White students sought quality academic programs and were concerned with how well their respective institutions ranked in comparison to other higher education institutions. The interviewees disclosed that Black college campuses provided small class sizes and strong faculty members who nurtured and mentored them and showed genuine interest in helping them to achieve their educational goals.

## Student Financial Support

Besides academic issues, Conrad et al. (1997) discovered that White students considered student scholarships and low tuition and fees as two important factors contributing to their continued enrollment at HBCUs. Funding a college education is a fundamental concern, and students in the study indicated that financial support often dictated whether they could pursue higher education and which institution they attended. Several interviewees emphasized that state-supported grants and programs designed to attract students of other races played a significant role in attracting them to Black college campuses. Students, faculty, and administrators agreed that scholarships are one of the best ways to attract and maintain White students. A student candidly declared, "I am here for the money. There's no way I would be here but for the money I am getting" (Conrad et al., 1997, p. 49). An administrator admitted that most White students attend Black colleges because the schools offer these students more money, and generally cost significantly less than predominantly White institutions. These findings attest to the power of money.

## Institutional Characteristics

The final category of factors that influence matriculation of White students in Black colleges includes: (a) positive image as a multiracial institution, (b) supportive and inclusive campus culture, (c) White student recruitment, (d) articulation and cooperative agreements with predominantly White institutions, (e) positive external relations with community and professional constituencies, (f) safe environment, and (g) attractive campus appearance (Conrad et al., 1997). Interviewees viewed the Black colleges as welcoming institutions and indicated that Black schools must make the general public aware that they are multiracial institutions to attract more White students. The White students in the study reported they desired a sense of comfort and selected Black colleges that demonstrate a culture of inclusiveness. The study showed that faculty, administrators, and students often referred to their respective campuses as a family unit.

Despite the advantages identified in the study, interviewees recognized that HBCUs must deliberately recruit White students. Due to the public perception that Black schools are reserved for Black students, many Whites are not aware of the access and opportunities available at these institutions. A few suggestions for altering this perception include recruitment visits to majority-White high schools, inviting White high school students to the campuses, and mailing brochures and other relevant information about HBCUs to White high school students (Conrad et al., 1997). Cooperative agreements established between predominantly White colleges and HBCUs aid in encouraging White students to attend Black colleges. Through articulation and cooperative agreements, the students enrolled in predominantly White schools are able to acquaint themselves with neighboring HBCUs by taking courses on their campuses. North Carolina A&T, for example, has successfully recruited White students from two-year colleges due to such agreements.

Moreover, Conrad et al. (1997) also found that the relationships of HBCUs and their surrounding communities and professional organizations influence the matriculation of White students. These relationships provide the schools with exposure to those students and others who are unfamiliar with them while simultaneously building connections with their local communities. Participants in the research study considered a safe campus environment, both on-campus and off-campus, as a fundamental concern. One administrator said that White students will enroll in Black colleges if the schools offer strong programs and the students feel secure in the learning environment. The final institutional characteristic that participants identified as an important factor is campus appearance. A campus with attractive buildings and groomed lawns, for example, lured White students. The study revealed that, for some interviewees, the aesthetics of the campus environment represented the college or university's reputation for quality.

The 14 factors identified by the researchers in this study provide insight into why White students choose to attend HBCUs. This information filled a void in a relatively unexplored area of higher education research. Discussion about the White presence on HBCUs started with the earlier works of sociologist Charles V. Willie (1981a, 1994); however, Conrad et al. (1997) explored this area of research further by conducting a systematic investigation. The multicase study design exhibited the researchers' engagement in what Brown (2003) identifies as the *emic* approach to examining Black colleges. The emic approach results when researchers invest the time and position themselves in Black college campuses with an acute awareness of the cultural implications embedded within the institutions. The researchers visited all five HBCUs and stayed on each campus one to two days. The scope of the research extended beyond the perspectives of the students to include faculty and administration. Including all three constituents (36 students, 12 faculty, and 32 administrators) strengthened the findings because it provided a more comprehensive view of why White students are attracted to HBCUs.

Overall, the researchers discovered that the factors influencing White students to attend Black colleges vary significantly from factors that influence white students to attend predominantly White institutions. The factors identified in this particular study serve as key suggestions to other Black colleges seeking to enroll more White students. Conrad et al. (1997) recommend: (a) enhancing the mission of the institutions by developing strong academic programs in competitive fields of study; (b) ensuring the presence of unique programs of study unavailable at nearby predominantly White institutions; and (c) increasing state funding to aid in institutional enhancement, student financial aid support, and recruitment. Although these suggestions are aimed at increasing matriculation of White students, they should be fundamental imperatives for HBCUs irrespective of the racial identity of the target student population. Ideally, Black colleges, like all other types of higher education institutions, should strive to be better equipped, more productive, and highly efficient. The reality, however, is that perhaps, with the focus shifting to White students, states will be more inclined to help Black colleges become more attractive institutions.

Charles V. Willie (1981a) addressed the matter of racial dynamics on Black college campuses by encouraging Black postsecondary schools to increase their White populations. He believed that White students should account for at least 20% of the student body at Black colleges and universities. He proposed that the monetary resources awarded to predominantly White institutions to recruit African American students should also be given to Black colleges and universities to recruit White students to their campuses. The idea is that, for desegregation to be successful in higher education, both predominantly White and HBCUs must deliberately take action to attract students of other races. His position stems from observing the positive impact minority status had on Dr. Benjamin E. Mays, an African American scholar and former president of Morehouse College, who earned two baccalaureate degrees from both an HBCU and a predominantly White college. Willie (1981a) describes Mays's immersion in the majority-White environment as a liberating experience in which he excelled in spite of his minority status and realized that White people were not superior beings. He deduced from this lesson that White people could also benefit from being part of the minority at Black colleges and universities. This experience at an HBCU provides White students the opportunity to interact with Black people, learn from them, and confront the negative stereotypes deeply embedded within their own consciousness. The anticipated result is that the experience will force White students to learn more about themselves and liberate them from the common belief that people of African decent should be separate *and* unequal.

In *Black Colleges Are Not Just for Blacks Anymore*, Willie (1994) continues to awaken the minds of individuals who believe that Black colleges are only beneficial to Black people. His introspective argument relies heavily on his identity as an African American man, a sociologist, and a Morehouse College alumnus. Additionally, he draws on his critical analysis and understanding of the academic literature on race, politics, sociology, and education. Willie (1994) suggests that White students attending Black colleges could develop what W.E.B. Du Bois identified as a double consciousness, which could enable them to gain a better self-concept while simultaneously learning how African Americans perceive them now that the tables have turned, and they are the minority. He recognizes that his position may not be popular among supporters of Black colleges and universities who fear that the infusion of a White student population will destroy the institutional culture of the schools. In response, Willie (1994) asserts:

> If the proof of the pudding is in the eating of it, the beneficial contributions of predominantly Black colleges and universities to the higher education system of this nation can be truthfully attested to only by individuals who have experienced it. For those who are leery of the wisdom of this proposal, let me remind you of the words of wise in-laws in the family. They always say at the wedding ceremony that they are not losing a daughter but gaining a son, or vice-versa. Diversity is the source of our salvation. The addition of White students to predominantly Black colleges and universities will strengthen, not weaken, them. The institutions that pursue this policy will not lose students but will gain new allies and friends. (p. 158)

This perspective suggests that White students do not pose a threat to the identity and legacy of Black schools. Willie (1994) views integration as a necessary step for all HBCUs to ensure their continued existence and progress.

Similar to Willie (1994), Brown (2002b) explores the issue of White students attending Black colleges. In a seminal study, *Good Intentions: Collegiate Desegregation and Transdemographic Enrollment*, Brown (2002b) explores the implications of White students attending public HBCUs. He conducted an ethnographic case study at Bluefield State University using artifact gathering, participant observation, document analysis, and informal interviews to collect data. The uniqueness of Bluefield State College is that, although federal regulation identifies it as an HBCU, the college maintains the lowest African American student enrollment and the highest White student enrollment of the nation's Black institutions of higher education. Additionally, the faculty is 92% White, and, at the time the study occurred, Bluefield State College was the only HBCU to have a White president.

In documenting and analyzing the significant changes that have taken place at Bluefield State University, Brown (2002b) coined the term *transdemography* to describe "shifts in the statistical composition of the student population within the corresponding institutions based solely on race" (p. 264). This is particularly important for public HBCUs because they are the primary targets of desegregation initiatives. Bluefield State University, however, is an example of collegiate desegregation gone awry (Drummond, 2000; Levinson, 2000). There are no Black Greek-letter organizations on campus, and most of the traditions "typical of an HBCU have vanished. There is no Greek life, no marching band, limited Black faculty/staff presence, and no signs of the historic traditions of the formerly Black-populated student body" (Brown, 2002b, p. 270).

While Bluefield State University intended to make its campus more diverse by increasing the number of White students, the Black population of students disappeared in the process. According to Brown (2002b), this transdemographic shift poses a survival conflict for public Black colleges. These institutions have to decide whether they will fulfill desegregation mandates and endure the consequences of losing their cultural identity or reject desegregation initiatives and risk legal penalty (Brown, 2002b).

The changes at Bluefield State University highlight the fear that often accompanies discussions of diversity at Black colleges. Even so, some critics continue to challenge the existence of these institutions, believing that these campuses inhibit establishment of the type of diversity they seek. The push toward making Black colleges more integrated institutions resonates in the book *Diversifying Historically Black Colleges and Universities: A New Higher Education Paradigm* (Sims, 1994). Sims approaches the issue of diversity from a more critical posture in which she asserts that Black colleges are maintaining segregated campus environments. The primary objective of the book is to provide faculty, staff, students, and administrators of HBCUs with a *how to* guide to increasing diversity. The use of the term *diversity* throughout Sims's (1994) book refers solely to the premise of increasing the presence of White students on HBCU campuses. She identifies the book *Two Nations: Black and White, Separate, Hostile, and Unequal* by Andrew Hacker as an influence in her decision to focus only on White students. Her position is that, although different ethnic groups exist, the dynamics between Black and White people are a more prevalent concern due to the long history of segregation and inequality between the two groups. Similar to Willie's (1981a/1994) work, Sims (1994) details the need for and benefits of diversity and why it is imperative for all HBCUs to take heed of what she identifies as the new higher education paradigm.

Diversity is not a new higher education topic. Most colleges and universities embrace the term *diversity* because it represents deliberate attempts at inclusiveness, access, and opportunity. Predominantly White institutions, in particular, regularly promote the value of making their campus populations more diverse and heavily recruit students of other races. The logic behind such initiatives stems partly from the genuine desire to do the right thing and make higher education a viable option for all people. The other part of the explanation is that higher education institutions cannot uphold the archaic doctrine of separate and unequal. Federal law requires colleges and universities to make their campuses more racially diverse. The push is for schools to embrace the concept of multiculturalism. Sims (1994) argues that the issue of diversity is somewhat problematic for HBCUs. She identifies it as the unspoken dilemma that Black institutions of higher education fail to address properly. Key stakeholders readily recognize the need to diversify Black schools, yet they fail to implement concrete plans to do so.

The dilemma of diversity remains unspoken because individuals invested in maintaining the legacy of Black colleges worry about the implications of recruiting White students. The concern again is what will happen to the rich cultural identity that has empowered Black students. According to Sims (1994), the advantages of diversifying Black colleges clearly outweigh the disadvantages of and concerns about disrupting the cultural aspect of Black college life. Diversity is a valuable tool that teaches tolerance and understanding. Diversifying Black colleges proves beneficial for the Black students enrolled and the White students recruited as both groups are able to learn from each other's experiences. The reoccurring message echoed throughout Sims's book is that the world is not just Black and White, and institutions of higher education should not be as well. The first step is convincing Black college stakeholders of the importance and necessity of diversifying their campuses by increasing the number of White students. The second, and perhaps more critical, step is showing HBCUs how to implement and maintain diversity initiatives.

The significance of Sims's (1994) work is that she provides a plan of action to aid Black colleges in their efforts to diversify their campuses. She suggests that the curriculum must be reformed and suited to the needs of a more diverse student population. The addition of courses focusing on other cultures and languages, for example, shows a commitment to diversity. Historically Black colleges and universities must aggressively recruit White students, and Sims (1994) proposes establishing special committees devoted solely to this mission. Recruitment materials, which should be directed to both White parents and students, must communicate that admission is open to all people, regardless of their race, sex, or disability. The objective is to make White students feel comfortable and safe in an environment where they are in the minority. The committee can also target junior high and high schools with predominantly White student populations and make them aware of the opportunities available at HBCUs. A helpful recruitment strategy is to include White students currently enrolled in Black colleges so prospective students are able to see individuals who look like them and who successfully function in an environment that is majority-African American. In addition to recruitment initiatives, Black colleges must be prepared to sustain their White student populations. Sims (1994) recommends that HBCUs restructure their campuses by implementing mandatory diversity workshops for faculty, creating support services that cater to the needs of White students, and modifying extracurricular activities so White students are able to participate in them.

The problem with most of the literature on diversity at HBCUs is that it often portrays these institutions as segregated and devoid of diversity. These depictions often provide a false representation of the Black college environment and ultimately contribute to the misconception that Black schools are reserved for Black people. Indeed, there is room for improvement in increasing diversity, and suggestions about how to do so are quite helpful. The problem is that HBCUs do not get credit for the diversity they do have. Willie (1981b) posits that diversity is present on Black college campuses in terms of the varying socioeconomic status of the student body. Historically Black colleges and universities attract students from both poor and privileged backgrounds who are placed in an environment in which they are forced to coexist. According to Willie (1981b), "Such diversity provides an inhospitable environment for the development of social class stereotypes" (p. 7). This type of diversity serves as a valuable learning tool for students as they are able to confront some of the stereotypes based on issues of class and status. The Black college campus serves as a platform for interaction, engagement, learning, and, ultimately, growth in understanding and tolerance.

## Profile of the American College President

In the history of American higher education, college and university presidents were traditionally White men selected from the clergy or other religious ministries (Cohen, 1998). Protestant religious denominations founded these institutions, and presidents were responsible for teaching ethics and moral philosophy. In response to the changing times, however, the presidential profile has evolved to be more science-driven and businesslike (Kauffman, 1980). Burton (2003) suggests that three recent trends have emerged over the years in regard to the college president. First, more institutions are hiring presidents outside faculty or academic ranks. Second, the path to the presidency is often complicated by issues of race, gender, and previous work experience. Third, more attention is given to the role of mentors and the importance of an institutional fit between the president and the institution.

Given the important role and far-reaching influence of the college president, it is important to know who these people are and how they attain these positions. Cohen and March (1986) examined the career path of presidents in their book, *Leadership and Ambiguity*. They identified the normative or traditional career ladder of college presidents, which involves a teaching or faculty appointment, followed by significant administrative experience. Previous administrative experience included serving as department chairperson, then dean, then vice president/provost for academic affairs.

In a more recent study, Birnbaum and Umbach (2001) also examine the career path of college presidents. The three primary questions of that study include: (a) What are the alternate career paths followed by college presidents? (b) Is there a relationship between career path and institutional type? (c) Is there a relationship between the career path and the personal characteristics of presidents? The 1995 American Council on Education (ACE) report on college and university presidents provided the data for this analysis.

In their research, Birnbaum and Umbach (2001) operationally defined the path of the presidents' careers as falling into two major categories, traditional and nontraditional. They coined the terms *steward* and *scholar* to refer to the normative career ladder developed by Cohen and March (1986). Scholar-presidents referred to those presidents who had held faculty positions and progressed through administrative appointments. The steward-president, on the other hand, did not have teaching experience and moved into the position strictly through the administrative path. The terms *spanner* and *stranger* were conceived in reference to the nontraditional category. According to Birnbaum and Umbach (2001), spanners were presidents who left the academy during some point in their career before assuming their position as president. Stranger-presidents, on the other hand, came from outside higher education and had no teaching experience.

Study findings indicated that approximately 89% of all presidents followed one of the traditional paths. Scholar-presidents account for 66.3% and stewards account for 22.4% of the sample studied. It is obvious, therefore, that the majority of presidents began their careers as faculty members and moved through the academic ranks into the presidency.

## African American Presidents and Administrators

Moving beyond issues of career trajectory, numerous research studies focus on African Americans and other people of color in higher education (Holmes, 2004). This racialized agenda indicates recognition that race influences how individuals experience various aspects of higher education. The majority of African American administrators work at HBCUs (Roebuck & Murty, 1993). Although few studies concentrate solely on presidents, they are often included in larger samples with other administrators.

Although he does not focus exclusively on college presidents, Hoskins (1978) produced a classic work on the status of Black administrators in higher education. The purpose of his study was to determine whether differences existed between Black administrators at predominantly Black institutions and Black administrators at predominantly White institutions. The differences examined included background characteristics, methods of recruitment and/or selection, and opinions toward and perceptions of employment. Administrators were selected from both Black land-grant institutions and White land-grant institutions, for a total population of 457. Participants were to be an assistant dean or higher. President was the highest academic office, and although only one responded from the predominantly White institutions, 18 responded from the predominantly Black ones. The researcher constructed a questionnaire and mailed it to all the identified Black administrators. The results of the study are divided into three categories: background characteristics, recruitment methods, and professional characteristics.

## Background Characteristics

The study revealed that background characteristics differed among institutions. For example, administrators at Black institutions were older than their colleagues at White institutions. Hoskins (1978) suggests that this finding could have serious implications for the future of Black institutions as these institutions may experience a shortage of trained Black professionals.

In terms of educational level, the findings confirmed no significant differences between the administrators. This particular finding is important, according to the researcher, because of the misguided assumption that Black institutions are inferior learning environments. The type of institution where the administrators received their undergraduate degrees varied significantly. Administrators at Black campuses generally attended Black institutions, and the majority of those at White institutions were educated at predominantly White colleges and universities. Both groups, however, received their advanced degrees (both at the master's and doctoral level) at White institutions. This finding is not surprising because of the lack of graduate programs at many Black institutions during the time of this study.

Comparing the administrators' religious preference revealed significant differences. The breakdown of administrators at Black institutions was: Protestant, 53.7%; Roman Catholic, 3.8%; Black Muslim, 0.5%; and other religious preference, 3.9%. The findings for administrators on predominantly

White campuses yielded: Protestant, 29.6%; Roman Catholic, 7.4%; Black Muslim, 0.00%; and other, 18.0% (Hoskins, 1978).

## *Methods of Recruitment and/or Selection*

Similar to background characteristics, administrators at Black colleges also experienced more diverse recruiting and selection procedures. Administrators at predominantly Black institutions remained in the same institution for many years and came up through the ranks to their current positions, and their responsibilities included teaching, raising funds for the institution, and administrative duties. Some of the administrators were recruited from other Black institutions. At White institutions, however, the majority of the administrators attained their positions by applying for vacancies. This finding does not suggest that recruitment of Black educators did not occur. According to Hoskins (1978), as soon as predominantly White institutions filled their predetermined quotas, they were more inclined to stop looking for any more Black candidates. In terms of learning about the position, at Black institutions, administrators learned of the position through friends or colleagues. Similarly, administrators at White institutions learned of their positions through acquaintances, but often to a lesser degree. Administrators at White institutions were often found through search and screening committees (Hoskins, 1978).

## *Professional Characteristics*

Administrators at predominantly Black institutions acquired higher rank than did administrators at White institutions. This finding is not surprising because many Black administrators were educated in Black schools and often remained at these institutions throughout their professional careers.

In terms of the type of students taught, no differences existed between the administrators of these institutions. Both taught undergraduates, graduates, and a combination of both. Although White institutions offered more graduate-level courses, administrators at Black college campuses taught significantly more than did their colleagues on predominantly White campuses. Tenure in position varied between administrators. Black administrators at Black schools had more seniority in their positions than did Black administrators at White schools. No significant differences were found in the amount of time devoted to teaching, research and writing, and administrative responsibilities (Hoskins, 1978).

Focusing on one particular type of administrator, Lewis (1988) conducted a study exploring the career development of African American college presidents. The objective of the study was to determine whether their career development was characterized by sponsored or contest mobility. Sponsored mobility refers to individuals who are selected early in their careers and are groomed and mentored into their occupational positions. Contest mobility, on the other hand, identifies those who are socialized to value competition and strategic planning as the means to attain career goals.

To gather data on the trajectory of African American college presidents, Lewis (1988) distributed a questionnaire concerning career mobility issues and educational, personal, and professional background information. The total population included 169 African American college presidents, and 93 questionnaires were returned for analysis. The researcher also conducted 20 follow-up interviews. The major findings of the study revealed that the average African American college president is a Black male between the ages of 50 and 59. Most of the presidents graduated from an HBCU or a predominantly Black higher education institution and pursued their graduate degrees at majority-White institutions. African American college presidents generally presided over four-year historically or predominantly Black institutions. The results also revealed that career development cannot be characterized solely as sponsored or contest mobility; most of the presidents experienced some degree of both (Lewis, 1988).

Holmes (2004) conducted a more recent qualitative study of African American presidents, *An Overview of African American College Presidents: A Game of Two Steps Forward, One Step Backward, and Standing Still*, whose purpose was to produce a profile of African American presidents in public and private institutions. More specifically, Holmes focused on finding the factors presidents considered to be most salient to their success and/or failure. Six presidents, three males and three females, agreed to participate. Based on the Carnegie classification system of 1994, the institutions in which they worked included one public doctorate-granting university, three public community colleges, and two baccalaureate institutions.

The researcher used semistructured interviews and asked participants about their career paths and issues pertaining to the impact of race. The findings revealed similar themes across institutional types. The presidents discussed the importance of family and its role in pushing them to achieve academically and further their collegiate-level education. Mentoring by other

colleagues was also cited as helpful in their adjustment and career development. Religious leaders and affiliation with religious organizations were also
recognized as a great source of comfort and encouragement. The presidents
varied in age ranging from 55 to 64, and all had children who earned college
degrees. In fact, three of them had children who were pursuing graduate or
professional degrees. Four of the presidents attended predominantly White
institutions throughout their educational process, and two attended Black
colleges for their undergraduate degree and predominantly White schools for
their graduate studies.

In terms of career path, two of the presidents were serving as college
president for the second time. The four remaining presidents held prior positions as vice president for academic affairs or dean of instruction. All six
presidents, however, held faculty positions in two- and four-year institutions
before serving as president. Based on the 2002 findings of the ACE study on
college presidents, Holmes (2004) found that African American administrators were similar to their White counterparts in terms of educational characteristics and prior administrative experiences.

Lindsay (1999) conducted a qualitative research study on African American women university executives, gathering information through semistructured interviews and an examination of school catalogues and other relevant
written documents on the institutions' mission statements and strategic
plans. The sample consisted of three presidents and one provost of both public and private universities located in various regions throughout the United
States. One university was identified as an HBCU.

The four women executives earned doctoral degrees from Research I institutions or reputable smaller schools, and they discussed the importance of
mentoring and how it had a positive effect on their careers. The women in
the study identified the critical role their mothers and other African American women leaders played in their career development, but they also stated
that it was difficult to have mentors as they climbed the administrative ladder
to the presidency because so few African American women occupy this position. The executives addressed the challenges they faced as African American
women in positions dominated by White men. Lindsay (1999) discovered a
pattern the women shared regarding expectations of their work and ability.
The women executives believed they had to exceed the responsibilities of
their jobs because more was expected from them than from White males in

similar positions. Despite this challenge, the women executives enjoyed serving as mentors and role models, particularly for young women.

## Presidents of Historically Black Colleges and Universities

Outside a few studies that look at the people who serve in these positions, the early literature on presidents of HBCUs rests solely on understanding their role in improving the conditions of their institutions. Most of the early researchers were African American educators with a vested interest in the success of education at Black institutions. Willie and MacLeish (1978) conducted a survey on presidents of Black colleges and asked the leaders about their priorities regarding the future direction of their institutions. Most of the participants said that educational matters were critical to the future success of HBCUs, including curriculum reform, faculty development, and implementation of new graduate programs. Financial matters ranked second in terms of importance. The presidents viewed increasing funds for student aid, research, faculty salaries, equipment, and library resources as necessary improvements. The presidents also suggested the need for Black institutions to improve in terms of management, particularly as it relates to recruiting more students, improving class registration procedures, and public relations.

In addition to management concerns, Willie and MacLeish (1978) inquired about the presidents' views toward racial integration of Black college campuses. The presidents emphasized that Black colleges have always been diverse at all institutional levels, including students, faculty, and administration. One president said, "Government actions to reverse the consequences of centuries of racial desegregation must not be used as an excuse to dismantle or change the orientation of the Black public colleges of the country" (Willie & MacLeish, 1978, p. 145). The presidents clearly recognized the value in making HBCUs more diverse and expanding access and opportunity to all individuals, regardless of race, creed, or national origin. However, they also expressed the need to maintain the historic roots of the institutions and not lose sight of the mission on which Black colleges were founded, the education of African American students.

Black college presidents are faced with numerous challenges, particularly in fiscal matters. The problems they face are severe, and the support they receive is scant (Willie & MacLeish, 1978). Prezell Robinson, former president of a Black institution, St. Augustine College, offers an introspective look into the president's role in managing scarce resources. He (1978) declares, "The tragedy of the inequity is that the American public, at large, seems to expect Black colleges to produce more with less than any other segment of American higher education" (as quoted in Willie & MacLeish, 1978, p. 158). This realization reflects the burden Black college presidents must overcome to ensure their institutions' survival. Based on his experiences as a president, Robinson suggests that presidents must have an effective board of trustees whose responsibilities include finding funding for the institution and establishing key objectives consistent with the institution's charter. The president does not work alone; however, as the chief academic officer, the president must demonstrate leadership skills and have the respect and confidence of the board of trustees, faculty, staff, and students. The overall responsibility of the Black college president is therefore to provide leadership, be a good fund-raiser and manager, and incorporate other administrators and faculty into the decision-making processes.

The most current and comprehensive study on presidents of HBCUs is a dissertation authored by Debra Buchanan (1988). Similar to earlier studies, the purpose of this study was to determine the important roles for presidents of Black colleges. The researcher also investigated the qualifications required of the position and examined both public and private institutions to find out whether the presidents maintained congruent perceptions.

In Buchanan's (1988) study, the researcher randomly selected four institutions (two public and two private) to investigate. In addition to the president, the academic vice president and the chair of the faculty senate or a senior faculty member were asked to participate. Although the presidents were the primary target, Buchanan (1988) solicited the varying perspectives to get a sense of how the role of the president was perceived by those outside it. Twelve people participated in the study, and each position was represented by four people. While the gender composition varied among the academic vice presidents and the senior faculty members, the sample of presidents consisted of all males. The researcher developed a questionnaire based on the assertions in the literature and conducted structured interviews.

Based on the research findings, the presidential roles considered most important include: (a) articulating a vision for the institution the position and examining both public and private institutions to find out if the presidents had congruent perceptions; (b) assembling an administrative team; (c) providing leadership during crisis; (d) planning for future directions; (e) managing resources; (f) providing a sense of unity to achieve common goals; (g) providing an environment conducive to leadership development; (h) securing financial support; and (i) shaping and reshaping institutional goals. The qualifications viewed as most valuable to aspiring presidents were separated into three groups: academic preparation, professional experience, and personal qualities. The most valuable academic fields included psychology, law, social sciences, and education, and professor, department chair, academic dean, and academic vice president were considered key professional experiences. The personal qualities perceived as being important were good communication and interpersonal skills, astuteness, possession of high energy, a focus on the future, and effective management skills. Both public and private Black colleges shared similar perceptions of the roles and qualifications of the presidents. The researcher attributed this congruence to the fact that HBCUs function in similar environments (Buchanan, 1988).

## Summary

The research makes clear that HBCUs are an integral component of the American higher education system. The various comments from myriad sources indicate interest in Black colleges, particularly as it relates to the more popular areas of Black college research, which include history, desegregation, students, faculty, and racial composition. The challenge is that the fundamental topic of mission remains overlooked. Many scholars implicitly examine mission, but few of them directly address the mission of HBCUs in a systematic manner. Many years ago, W.E.B. Du Bois and Booker T. Washington initiated the debate on the mission of historically Black colleges, yet current scholarship neglects to address it thoroughly.

# 3

## PROFILES OF SELECTED
## BLACK COLLEGES

T he general historic mission of Black colleges and universities is well documented in the academic literature: these institutions were created to educate African Americans. Now, it is imperative to look beyond this celebrated mission to ascertain the current status of these institutions. For the purposes of the study, mission is not confined to the official mission statements cited in college and university websites, catalogues, and recruitment brochures. Extensive research targeting the presidency at two-year colleges suggests that presidents of these particular institutions serve a unique function, and that the issues facing two-year and four-year colleges and universities are significantly different (Kubala, 1999; McFarlin, Crittenden, & Ebbers, 1999; Phelps, Taber, & Smith, 1996; Vaughan & Weisman, 1997). The focus of this book is on four-year institutions because they represent the majority of the historically Black colleges and universities (HBCUs) in the United States.

This chapter examines how presidents of four-year HBCUs view the missions of their institutions. First, thorough profiles of both the HBCUs and the presidents sampled for the study establish the context of the research findings. In addition to seeking answers to the specific research questions posed, an equally important objective of the study is to bring attention to and focus on Black colleges and the presidents who lead them. Before gaining the presidents' perspectives on what constitutes their schools' missions, the study would be remiss without careful examination of who they are as individuals and the details that distinguish one HBCU from the next.

The information provided comes primarily from interviews with the presidents, coupled with investigation of the various HBCU official school websites. The presidents varied in terms of how responsive they were to the interview questions, and the Black colleges varied in terms of how much information they included on their websites. Consequently, the scope of the profiles differs. Despite the varying levels of information provided, the study acknowledges the contributions of the 15 participating presidents and schools (see Table 3.1). Although numerous studies focus on college presidents in general, presidents of HBCUs are either included in the periphery or are omitted completely from the discussion. Accordingly, the study moves beyond the profile of credentials and offers a more personal account of the presidents' paths to their positions. This study also provides a platform for presidents of Black colleges to tell their stories and showcase their respective institutions. The study used pseudonyms to replace the names of both the presidents and the schools to protect their identities, as agreed on in the letter of informed consent.

Second, this chapter details the presidents' responses to the specific research questions posed: (a) how they define the mission of their respective

**TABLE 3.1**
**Profile of Historically Black Colleges and Universities in the Study\***

| Institution | President | Sector | Founding Year | Student Enrollment |
|---|---|---|---|---|
| Morrison State University | Dr. Clarence Myers | Public | Early 1900s | 4,000 |
| Jemison State University | Dr. Scales Donahoo | Public | Late 1800s | 5,000 |
| Bassett State University | Dr. Bobby Isaac | Public | Late 1800s | 5,000 |
| Tubman University | Dr. Nathan Dudley | Private | Mid-1900s | 450 |
| Giovanni State University | Dr. Sultan Rovaris | Public | Late 1800s | 3,000 |
| University of Angelou | Dr. Mathilda Marie | Public | Late 1800s | 3,775 |
| Scott King College | Dr. Earl Davis | Private | Mid-1800s | 950 |
| Winfrey College | Ms. Mary Frances | Private | Mid-1800s | 975 |
| Chisholm State University | Mr. Devon Lamard | Public | Early 1800s | 1,550 |
| Hurston State University | Dr. Jared Auguste | Public | Late 1800s | 2,500 |
| Walker University | Dr. Trevis Freeman | Public | Late 1800s | 3,000 |
| Shabazz University | Dr. Kerry Foster | Public | Mid-1800s | 8,350 |
| Brooks University | Dr. Acosta Lee | Public | Mid-1900s | 4,000 |
| Waters University | Dr. Lyelle Boutte | Public | Late 1800s | 3,500 |
| Height University | Dr. John Spencer | Public | Early 1900s | 7,700 |

\*Pseudonyms replace the names of the college or university and the president.

institutions, (b) their role in implementing the mission, and (c) significant barriers that hinder mission implementation. The assertion is that Black colleges have a distinct organizational culture due to the minority population they primarily serve. Presidents of HBCUs have a comprehensive understanding of how these institutions function, so they are able to provide valuable insight into their role in the larger system of American higher education.

Finally, the chapter concludes with the presidents' perspectives on the current state of HBCUs as a whole. Black colleges face many similar challenges, and their presidents, as leaders of these institutions, share similar experiences. They offer their views on pressing concerns, including (a) whether Black colleges and universities serve a unique mission compared to other types of higher education institutions, (b) the relevance of the historic mission of educating African Americans, and (c) the overall importance of HBCUs.

## Profile of Participating Historically Black Colleges and Universities

Contrary to popular belief, HBCUs are not all the same. Indeed, they share a similar history and perhaps similar challenges, but Black colleges possess their own identities and unique characteristics in addition to their own strengths and weaknesses. The following descriptions seek to profile the Black colleges and universities represented in the study as distinct higher education institutions. The profiles include information on historical development, student enrollment, degree offerings, and other relevant attributes of the HBCUs that participated in the study.

### *Morrison State University*

Morrison State University is a public, comprehensive, liberal arts, higher education institution founded in the early 1900s. The school is located in an urban, metropolitan city in the northeastern United States. The university developed as a normal school whose primary function was to prepare school teachers. Thirty-eight years after its founding, Morrison State's curriculum expanded, and the institution began to offer baccalaureate degrees in areas other than teacher education. Currently the school remains as the only higher education institution in the state to manage a public school. Morrison State offers 53 undergraduate programs and nine master's degree programs, which include evening, weekend, and distance-learning courses. Approximately 4,000 students make up the campus population, and the most popular majors include nursing, education, and social work.

## Jemison State University

Jemison State University developed in the late 1800s as a land-grant institution under the provisions of the Second Morrill Act of 1890. Originally referred to as a *Colored Institute*, Jemison State's early curriculum centered on teacher preparation and vocational training. As a result of *Brown v. Board of Education*, however, the public school transitioned into a predominantly White institution with an older student population. Jemison State, located on the East Coast, has approximately 5,000 students and offers 22 undergraduate programs in criminal justice, business, teacher education, and social work. The school has two master's level programs, in biotechnology and media studies. Additionally, Jemison State enables students to enroll in preprofessional programs in dentistry, law, medicine, engineering, and pharmacy.

## Bassett State University

Founded in the late 1800s as the only school in the state that educated African Americans, Bassett State University, a land-grant institution, combines liberal arts and vocational training. The school, located in a small town in the southern United States, currently enrolls 5,000 students, and some of its most popular majors are education, accounting, computer science, and political science. Students choose from 54 undergraduate programs, 12 graduate programs, and 18 teacher certification programs. Bassett State retains the distinction of being the only higher education institution in the state to offer an undergraduate nuclear engineering program and a doctor of education degree.

## Tubman University

Tubman University is a private, Christian graduate school of theology. The school, established in the mid-1900s, represents a consortium of several religious denominations, including Baptist, United Methodist, African Methodist Episcopal, Christian Methodist Episcopal, Presbyterian, and Church of God in Christ. Tubman is located in a major metropolitan city in the southern United States. It enrolls approximately 450 students and offers both master's- and doctoral-level degrees.

## *Giovanni State University*

Giovanni State University is a land-grant institution chartered in the late 1800s. This comprehensive, liberal arts school began as an industrial high school and achieved university status in the late 1900s. Giovanni State is located in a relatively small town in the southern United States. Students choose from more than 50 academic majors, and the institution offers master's degrees in education and counseling, public health, and animal science. The school enrolls 3,000 students, 94% of whom are African American. Giovanni State sends more African American students to dental and medical schools than any other institution in its state.

## *University of Angelou*

University of Angelou, a land-grant institution established in the late 1800s, was first known as an academy. This liberal arts institution maintains a strong connection with the Methodist Episcopal Church. In the mid-1940s, the school transitioned into a college and later attained university status. Angelou is in the northeastern quadrant of the United States; currently enrolls approximately 3,775 students; and offers baccalaureate degrees in 26 disciplines, 13 teaching programs, and 8 preprofessional programs. In addition to the host of master's degrees it offers, Angelou offers the doctor of philosophy in organizational leadership, toxicology, food science and technology, and marine estuarine and environmental science.

## *Scott King College*

Scott King College, which dates back to the mid-1800s, began as a seminary and conferred its first bachelor's degrees in the late 1800s. This private, liberal arts institution offers 23 majors and minors at the undergraduate level in a variety of areas, including accounting, education, biology, chemistry, and mathematics. Scott King is located in the state's capital city in the northeastern United States. Currently the school enrolls approximately 950 students and provides course offerings during the evenings and on weekends. Scott King maintains strong ties to the United Methodist Church.

## *Winfrey College*

Winfrey College, chartered in the mid-1800s, began as a teacher training school. This private, liberal arts school sits on a former plantation in a southern state. Winfrey conferred its first bachelor's degrees in the early 1900s and currently offers undergraduate degrees in the humanities, natural sciences, social sciences, and education. The school preserves a strong Christian foundation as it provides educational opportunities to nearly 975 students.

### Chisholm State University

Chisholm State University, originally a teachers college, was established in the early 1800s. The Quakers helped to build this public, liberal arts institution, which attained university status in the late 1900s. The school offers baccalaureate degrees in more than 30 disciplines and master's degrees in education. While teaching remains a popular profession among Chisholm State students, they also major in business, medicine, communications, and government services. Currently Chisholm State serves approximately 1550 students.

### Hurston State University

Hurston State University, a land-grant institution, was founded in the late 1800s. Originally termed an Industrial College for Colored Youth, Hurston State is the oldest public Black college in its southern state. It became a degree-granting institution in the early 1900s. The school is located in a city with a population of 137,000. Current student enrollment is 2,500, and the student-faculty ratio is approximately 16:1. Hurston State offers 22 undergraduate majors and master's degrees in public administration, marine science, and social work. Additionally, Hurston State is the only school in the region to offer a four-year naval Reserve Officers' Training Corps (ROTC) program.

### Walker University

Founded in the late 1800s as a land-grant institution, Walker University is located in a rural community in the southern United States. Walker awarded its first bachelor's degrees in the early 1900s, and it remains the only HBCU in the state. The estimated current student enrollment is 3,000. Walker offers master's-level programs in rehabilitation counseling and education and doctorates in physical therapy. This liberal arts institution is known particularly for its research on goats.

### Shabazz University

Shabazz University, a land-grant institution, was founded in the mid-1800s as a training ground for future teachers of color. The school granted its first

B.S. degree in the early 1900s, and it is the second-oldest school in this southern state. Currently Shabazz enrolls approximately 8,350 students and offers 39 undergraduate majors, 31 master's degree options, and four doctoral programs. Shabazz regularly produces a number of nurses, engineers, and educators.

### Brooks University

In the mid-1900s, Brooks University was established as a branch campus of a larger college system. This public, liberal arts school opened its doors for instruction as an independent institution in 1959. Located in a southern metropolitan area, Brooks currently enrolls 4,000 students, and its most popular undergraduate majors include education, business administration, social work, and criminal justice. It also offers graduate instruction in computer information systems, criminal justice, education in urban schools, and social work at the master's level.

### Waters State University

Waters State University, a public, liberal arts institution, was founded in the late 1800s as a Black teachers college. It conferred its first bachelor's degrees in the early 1900s and was integrated after *Brown v. Board of Education.* Current student enrollment is approximately 3,500, and most students are White. Located on the East Coast, Waters State offers both baccalaureate and associate degrees in nursing, computer science, accounting, and education, among others.

### Height University

Height University, founded in the early 1900s, opened its doors as a religious training school in the southern United States. Although originally chartered as a private school, Height was the first state-supported, liberal arts college for African Americans in the nation. This public institution, which originally focused primarily on training teachers and preparing principals, now enrolls approximately 7,700 students majoring in nursing and such preprofessional programs as medicine, law, and dentistry. Height offers master's degrees in education, business administration, information science, library science, and public administration, and it has its own school of law.

## Campus Contexts and Observations

Historically Black colleges and universities share a common ancestry. All of them developed to educate African Americans at a time when Black people did not have educational access or opportunity. Early on, they all focused on religious training and teacher preparation; however, all of them transitioned from secondary schools into degree-granting higher education institutions. Despite these similarities, the profiles of the 15 HBCUs included in this study reveal the following distinctions that reflect their diversity:

1. Six of the 15 Black colleges began as land-grant institutions.
2. Twelve of the schools are public, and three are private.
3. The HBCUs are dispersed across 11 states in the southern and northeastern United States.
4. Two of the Black colleges offer only baccalaureate degrees, and five of them offer doctoral degrees.
5. The number of students enrolled in the schools varies from 450 to 8,350.
6. Two of the HBCUs serve a predominantly White student population.
7. The total sample of schools offers a variety of academic majors, including nursing, education, computer science, nuclear engineering, biotechnology, and such preprofessional programs as law, dentistry, medicine, and pharmacy.

## Profile of Presidents in the Study

Most of the research available on HBCUs focuses on two key constituents, students and faculty. Administrators, particularly presidents, receive minimal attention in the academic literature. Consequently, there is no work profiling this particular cohort of leaders.

The interest in college presidents stems partly from their status as elites, individuals of rank, power, and influence who evoke curiosity, wonder, mystique (Dexter, 1970; Hertz & Imber, 1995; Moyser & Wagstaffe, 1987; Thomas, 1995). The fascination with elites usually centers on who they are as individuals and how they were able to attain such a position. This section of the study addresses this fascination and presents profiles of the participating HBCU presidents (see Table 3.2). The first interview question asked presidents, "Can you tell me about yourself and how you arrived at the college presidency?" Although this was a warm-up question, it became a significant part of the research findings. To the researchers' surprise, the presidents provided more detail than anticipated. They spoke candidly and some at length about their experiences. The information is relevant because, without careful consideration and systematic investigation of these leaders, the literature does not have a holistic view of Black colleges in America and their leadership.

The following profiles provide an overview of the presidents' trajectory including their educational background, prior work experience, and other relevant information.

### Dr. Clarence Myers

Dr. Myers was appointed president of Morrison State University in March 2003. He earned a bachelor's degree in sociology from Springfield College; two master's degrees, one in social work from the University of Connecticut and one in public health from the University of Pittsburgh; and a doctoral degree in social welfare policy from the University of Pittsburgh. Dr. Myers worked at Carnegie Mellon University and the University of Minnesota as an assistant professor and then held appointments in the University of Connecticut's School of Social Work, School of Allied Health, and School of Medicine. During his time at the University of Connecticut, he achieved full professor status in eight years and transitioned into the position of associate dean for research and development. Dr. Myers served as vice president for academic affairs at Eastern Connecticut State University, and, before assuming the presidency at Morrison State, served as vice chancellor of student and multicultural affairs at the University of Wisconsin-Milwaukee.

### Dr. Scales Donahoo

Dr. Donahoo, the ninth president of Jemison State University, earned a B.S. in English from Tennessee State University and an M.S. in journalism from the University of Illinois at Urbana-Champaign where he worked as a public information officer for the Department of Mental Health, after which he returned to school and acquired an Ed.D. in higher education administration from George Peabody College for Teachers of Vanderbilt University. After graduation, Dr. Donahoo completed postdoctoral studies at Carnegie

**TABLE 3.2**
**Profile of Presidents in the Study***

| President | Inauguration | Undergraduate Institution | Undergraduate Major | Graduate Institution | Highest Degree Completed |
|---|---|---|---|---|---|
| Dr. Clarence Myers | 2003 | Springfield College | Sociology | University of Pittsburgh | Ph.D. |
| Dr. Scales Donahoo | 1987 | Tennessee State University | English | Vanderbilt Peabody College | Ed.D. |
| Dr. Bobby Isaac | 2004 | "Bassett" State University | Mathematics | Michigan State | Ph.D. |
| Dr. Nathan Dudley | 2004 | Trinity College | Sociology | Howard University | D.Min. |
| Dr. Sultan Rovaris | 2001 | Oberlin College | Economics | Stanford University | Ph.D. |
| Dr. Mathilda Marie | 2002 | Howard University | English | Howard University | Ph.D. |
| Dr. Earl Davis | 2005 | University of Georgia | Biology | Georgia State University | Ph.D. |
| Ms. Mary Frances | 2002 | "Winfrey" College | Psychology | Jackson State University | M.A. |

| Mr. Devon Lamard | 2004 | Hampton University | Industrial Education | George Washington University | M.A. |
| Dr. Jared Auguste | 1997 | University of Massachusetts Amherst | English | University of Massachusetts, Amherst | Ed.D. |
| Dr. Trevis Freeman | 1979 | "Walker" University | Education | University of Oklahoma | Ph.D. |
| Dr. Kerry Foster | 2003 | University of Kentucky | History | Duke University | Ph.D. |
| Dr. Acosta Lee | 2002 | Morehouse College | Chemistry | Howard University | Ph.D. |
| Dr. Lyelle Boutte | 2002 | Lincoln University of Missouri | Elementary Education | Indiana University, Bloomington | Ed.D. |
| Dr. John Spencer | 2001 | Florida A&M University | Political Science | Florida State University | Ph.D. |

*Pseudonyms replace the names of the presidents.

Mellon University. He worked at Norfolk State University, an HBCU, as executive assistant to the president, assistant vice president for student affairs, and vice president for student affairs. Dr. Donahoo achieved tenure status as an associate professor of journalism during his time at Norfolk State University. He later served as president of Philander Smith College, an HBCU in Little Rock, Arkansas, before becoming the president of Jemison State in September 1987.

### Dr. Bobby Isaac

Dr. Isaac, the ninth president of Bassett State University, earned B.S. in mathematics and an M.Ed. from Bassett State University. He later earned a Ph.D. in higher education from Michigan State University. While at Michigan State, Dr. Isaac was an institutional research analyst and assistant professor. He later returned to Bassett State, where he held numerous positions, including research fellow, assistant director of the Institutional Self-Study, director of the Institutional Self-Study, and assistant vice president for academic affairs. Dr. Isaac then decided to return to the classroom and was a professor of mathematics for 16 years. He accepted the position of interim executive vice president prior to assuming his role as president of Bassett State in July 2004.

### Dr. Nathan Dudley

Dr. Dudley, who was appointed the seventh president of Tubman University in September 2004, earned a bachelor's degree from Trinity College, a Master of Divinity from Duke University, and a Doctor of Ministry from Howard University, an HBCU. His career began at another HBCU, Hampton University, where he served as dean of the Chapel and chairman of the religious affairs department. During his time at Hampton, Dr. Dudley taught religion and philosophy for more than 20 years. He moved on to Virginia State University as a professor in the philosophy department and became associate vice president of student affairs. Dr. Dudley also worked at Chicago State University, a predominantly Black institution, as vice president of student affairs before taking over the presidency at Tubman University.

### Dr. Sultan Rovaris

Dr. Sultan studied economics as an undergraduate at Oberlin College. He earned a master's degree in education from Cleveland State University and went on to Stanford University, where he earned a second master's degree and a Ph.D. in higher education administration. He began his career teaching at the University of California at Santa-Cruz and moved to the State University of New York at Buffalo, where he was promoted to associate professor. Dr. Rovaris went on to Louisiana State University to become department chair and was promoted to full professor. At Medgar Evers College, he became vice president for academic affairs. Dr. Rovaris was appointed the seventh president of Giovanni State University in October 2001.

## Dr. Mathilda Marie

Dr. Marie, who was appointed the 13th president of the University of Angelou in 2002, began her pursuit of higher education at Howard University, where she majored in English and earned a B.A., M.A., and Ph.D. Dr. Marie started her career as a faculty member teaching English at City University of New York and two HBCUs, Bowie State University and the University of the District of Columbia. In addition to her responsibilities as a professor at the University of the District of Columbia, she served as assistant chair of the English department and associate dean of the College of Liberal and Fine Arts. Before assuming the presidency at University of Angelou, she was academic vice president of Norfolk State University.

## Dr. Earl Davis

Appointed the 12th president of Scott King College in December 2005, Dr. Davis earned a B.S. in biology from the University of Georgia, an M.S. in college student personnel services from Miami University, and a Ph.D. in higher education from Georgia State University. He started his career as coordinator of Greek life at Emory University and then was named assistant director of student activities at Georgia State University. Dr. Davis has also served as director of student activities at Old Dominion University and vice president for student affairs at Albany State University. He is the youngest president of any HBCU.

## Mary Frances

Ms. Frances, the first female president of Winfrey College, received a bachelor's degree in psychology there. She enrolled in another HBCU, Jackson State University, where she earned her master's degree in public policy administration. Ms. Frances is currently pursuing her doctorate in organizational management and leadership. At the start of her career, she served as executive director of the Mental Health Association, executive director for the governor's office of federal state programs, and commissioner for the state's group on workers compensation. Ms. Frances returned to Winfrey College in a dual role as executive assistant to the president and director of the Health and Wellness Center. She later accepted the position of vice president for institutional advancement and then was appointed interim president. In May 2002, she became Winfrey's 13th president.

## Devon Lamard

Mr. Lamard, interim president of Chisholm State University since January 2004, has a B.S. in industrial education from Hampton University and an M.A. in personnel management and administration from George Washington University. He dedicated 34 years of his professional career to the U.S. Army and was commander of the national ROTC. Mr. Lamard retired from the military as a major general and spent six years in managerial jobs in private industry and information technology business. He returned to his alma mater, Hampton University, as director of the Data Conversion and Management Laboratory and later assumed the role of interim president of Chisholm State.

## Dr. Jared Auguste

Dr. Auguste, 11th president of Hurston State University, earned a bachelor's degree in English with a minor in American studies from the University of Massachusetts at Amherst. He also completed his Ed.D. in multicultural education with a focus on organizational change at University of Massachusetts at Amherst. Dr. Auguste began his career as a faculty member at Old Dominion University and remained there until he acquired tenure. He joined the faculty at Hampton University, where he served as dean of the School Liberal Arts and Education and, later, vice president for planning and dean of the Graduate College. Dr. Auguste assumed the presidency of Hurston State University in July 1997.

## Dr. Trevis Freeman

Dr. Freeman's appointment as the 14th president of Walker University occurred in October 1979. He received his bachelor's degree from Walker University, master's degree from Oklahoma State University, and doctorate in higher education from the University of Oklahoma. Dr. Freeman studied for two summers at the University of California at Berkeley and then spent a year on a National Science Foundation fellowship at Ohio State University. He arrived at Walker as a biology professor and assistant registrar. A year later he became the registrar full time and then dean of student affairs, a position he held for nearly 10 years. Dr. Freeman served as interim president before being appointed president of Walker. His status as President Emeritus is pending.

### Dr. Kerry Foster

Dr. Foster assumed the presidency at Shabazz University in August 2003, has bachelor's and master's degrees in history from the University of Kentucky and a doctorate in history from Duke University. He has served as professor and provost at both Duke University and the University of Texas at Arlington. Before assuming the presidency of Shabazz University, he was executive vice president for academic affairs and provost at the University of Texas at Arlington.

### Dr. Acosta Lee

Dr. Lee, president of Brooks University, received a B.S. in chemistry from Morehouse College and a master's and Ph.D. in physical chemistry from Howard University (both of these are HBCUs). He became full professor of chemistry at Southern University and A&M College, another HBCU. Dr. Lee accepted the position of associate vice chancellor for academic affairs before becoming interim and then, in May 2002, president.

### Dr. Lyelle Boutte

Dr. Boutte was appointed the 12th president of Waters University in September 2002. He attended Lincoln University of Missouri, an HBCU, where he earned a bachelor's degree in elementary education. He then went to Bradley University and earned three master's degrees in elementary education, educational administration, and secondary education/community college education. At Indiana University-Bloomington, he attained an Ed.D. in educational administration with a minor in business administration. Dr. Boutte went to Lincoln University of Missouri, where he was a professor and associate dean of education, and later held administrative posts at three additional HBCUs: dean at North Carolina A&T State University, provost at Harris-Stowe State University, and vice chancellor for academic affairs at Elizabeth City State University.

### Dr. John Spencer

Dr. Spencer has been president of Height University since June 2001. He attended Florida A&M University, an HBCU, where he earned a bachelor's degree in political science. He then earned a master's degree and doctor of philosophy from Florida State University. Dr. Spencer started as a faculty member teaching public policy, public administration, and political science at the University of Central Florida. He remained there for six years and then returned to Florida A&M University as a professor of political science. In addition, he accepted the position of assistant vice president of academic affairs and moved up the ranks to provost before assuming the presidency of Height University in June 2001.

## Presidential Backgrounds and Observations

The preceding profiles detail the unique experiences and characteristics of the presidents participating in the study. This information is particularly interesting because of the lack of previous investigative inquiry targeting this group of leaders and because it provides a more concrete representation of who these individuals are and how they ascended to the presidency. The participants' varied experiences revealed the following key similarities and differences among the presidents in their backgrounds, educational attainments, and work experience:

1. All of the presidents are of African descent.
2. Two of the presidents are female, and 13 are male.
3. Thirteen of the presidents earned doctoral degrees, including the Ph.D., Ed.D., and D.Min. Two of the presidents received master's degrees as their highest degree.
4. Nine of the presidents received bachelor's degrees from HBCUs.
5. Three of the presidents earned doctoral degrees from HBCUs, and one earned bachelor's, master's, and doctoral degrees from Black colleges.
6. Although the programs of study differed among the presidents, five of the 15 participants earned doctorates in higher education or higher education administration.

7. Before occupying the presidency, 11 of the 15 participants had worked on Black college campuses in varied capacities.

8. Two of the presidents have spent their entire careers solely at HBCUs.

9. One president has dedicated his higher education career to one HBCU, his undergraduate alma mater. Currently he is pending the status of President Emeritus.

10. Four of the participants had never worked at an HBCU setting before being appointed president. These four presidents did not attend a Black college as an undergraduate or graduate student.

11. Only one of the participants had served as president—an HBCU—before his current appointment.

12. Twelve of the presidents have held their position for less than five years, and two have served long tenures; one is approaching 19 years and the other has served almost 27 years.

So what does this information reveal about presidents of Black colleges? Perhaps the most obvious observation is that a strong correlation exists between individuals who attend and work at Black colleges and those who attain the presidency. Sixty percent of the sample earned bachelor's degrees from an HBCU, while 73% of the participants worked on a Black college campus prior to becoming president. This information suggests that HBCUs have a boomerang effect that provides individuals with the incentive to return. Dr. Clarence Myers, for example, was aware of this correlation. He did not attend an HBCU, nor did he work at one before applying for the presidency at Morrison State University. He said, "I was considered for the presidency at two other schools and I was surprised to get this one because I didn't attend an HBCU and HBCUs generally want their own" (personal communication, July 7, 2005).

Overall, the majority of presidents of Black colleges follow what Cohen and March (1986) identify as the normative or traditional career route. More specifically, 87% of the presidents fit into the category of what Birnbaum and Umbach (2001) refer to as scholar-presidents. Scholars are those presidents who held previous faculty positions and progressed up the administrative ladder. The study participants taught courses in various disciplines such as journalism, mathematics, philosophy, biology, political science, and chemistry, and the administrative positions included assistant director of student activities, associate dean of education, associate vice chancellor for academic affairs, vice president for student affairs, and vice president for academic affairs, to name a few. The presidents in the study shared the following thoughts concerning their career patterns:

> I took the traditional route. I was an assistant professor, an associate, then full. I was a vice president for academic affairs and a vice chancellor for student affairs. Yeah, it's somewhat old fashioned, and I recognize that there are other routes, like straight administration. But I firmly believe in academic rigor, and there's no substitute for that. (Dr. Clarence Myers, personal communication, July 7, 2005)

> I love research and scholarship and investigation and things of that nature. I kind of moved through the ranks, and in our profession if you are a good teacher, you become the department chair, and if you are good at chairs you become deans. If you are good at the deanship, you become vice president and then president, and that is what happened to me. (Dr. Mathilda Marie, personal communication, July 29, 2005)

> I began to map the traditional route to the presidency: assistant professor, associate professor, tenure, full professor, department chair, dean, vice president, and then president. I surmised that because of the color of my skin I should probably follow the traditional route so that people could not use that against me. (Dr. Sultan Rovaris, personal communication, August 15, 2005)

The overwhelming sentiment of the responses indicates that the majority of Black college presidents value and recommend the traditional or old-fashioned route to the presidency. The participants stressed the importance of being in the classroom and working directly with students and saw teaching as a prerequisite to being an effective administrator. Nevertheless, 13% of the sample fit into what Cohen and March (1986) identify as the nontraditional path, and one of the participating presidents is a steward-president.

According to Birnbaum and Umbach (2001), a steward-president is a president without teaching experience who moves up the ranks through administrative appointments. The lone steward-president in the study is a woman who worked primarily in state government and then transitioned to lower-level academic administration before attaining the presidency. The other nontraditional president fits into the category of what Birnbaum and

Umbach (2001) refer to as the stranger-president, one who has no experience in a higher education environment. The stranger-president in the sample spent his entire career in the military prior to becoming interim president. Devon Lamard offered the following:

> The road that I have followed to this position today has probably been one that is a little unusual, that is somewhat different. But in terms of what someone might consider qualifications or background for the position and all those sorts of things, I think that all my years of leadership and significant managerial responsibility in government and in private industry has prepared me to do leadership and management on a university campus. So I don't feel like a fish out of water by any means at all in terms of the leader responsibilities and managerial responsibilities that I have for people, for resources, for infrastructure, for planning ahead for development, all those things that are so key and essential on the university campus. (personal communication, August 16, 2005)

This perspective broadens the expectation of what constitutes a college president and sheds light on the fact that all individuals do not have to follow an established path to attain the presidency. While the traditional route is the most popular, the nontraditional presidents were unapologetic for their background and experience and were steadfast in their belief that they were qualified for and deserving of the position. In fact, the steward-president made school history when she became the first woman president in her institution's history. This accomplishment alone suggests that nontraditional does not equate to wrong or less than necessary. The nontraditional path simply means different or taking the road less traveled. The path to the presidency, however, involves more than academic degree attainment and prior work experience.

## Path to the Presidency: Beneath the Credentials

The college presidency is a rather exclusive position. As evidenced in the presidential profiles, the position does not require a specific academic major or an absolute work record, although clearly certain levels of credentials are necessary because of the demanding responsibilities of the job (Kauffman, 1980). The study participants, however, revealed other dimensions to their journeys. They emphasized other influences that played a major role in structuring their careers toward the presidency. This section of the study provides a more intimate look into their experiences by examining the path beneath their credentials.

## The Path: Planned or Unintentional

Eighty percent of the presidents in the study said the college presidency was an unintentional career move. According to Dr. Scales Donahoo, "My initial career goal was to become a VP [vice president] for student affairs by the time I was 41 and I think in terms of how my career moved, that happened when I was 32. I just never thought about being a college president . . ." (personal communication, July 7, 2005). Many of the participants shared this experience. They did not aspire to be college presidents because most of them enjoyed their roles as professors and high-level administrators. The one position, however, the majority of the participants aspired to was vice president for student affairs. This position appeared to represent the pinnacle of their academic career aspirations. The presidents engaged in behavior evincing sponsored mobility, which means that they were groomed and mentored into the position of president.

Conversely, 20% of the study participants reported that they planned early on in their careers to be college presidents. According to Dr. Earl Davis, "It was very intentional in terms of wanting to be a president . . . in terms of the preparation and things I knew I needed to do: get a Ph.D., to be involved in some teaching, do some research, all those things involved in professional associations I knew I needed to do all those things so it was very intentional" (personal communication, August 2, 2005). Individuals who wanted to be president positioned themselves and structured their careers accordingly. They engaged in what Lee (1988) identifies as contest mobility, which refers to career development as an experience involving a competitive spirit and strategic planning.

## The Choice: Why Lead a Black College?

The American higher education system comprises many types of colleges and universities, so why lead a Black college? The study asked the participants, "Why did you choose to become a president of an HBCU? Was it conscious choice to lead a Black institution of higher education?" The following are a few informative responses:

It was [a conscious choice]. Again, being a graduate of an HBCU and having worked at Florida A&M for 18 years, I have a deep love and respect for our institutions and what we do. When I look at colleges and universities across America, we need to ensure that we have a continuous stream of enlightened leadership at the helm. . . . I thought I had something significant to contribute to HBCUs, and again with my background, coming from a single-parent home . . . with limited resources . . . people like that need champions, and I think that I can do that, and so that's the special appeal to me to be a part of these institutions. (Dr. John Spencer, personal communication, August 19, 2005)

HBCUs are the best shot at getting African American students through. They have a better sense of support, and they are nurturing institutions. . . . All Black people do not have to attend an HBCU in order to get an education or to be successful. It is a matter of choice. (Dr. Clarence Myers, personal communication, July 7, 2005)

Well, it was a conscious choice to work at a historically Black college or university . . . I think that the work that these institutions do is so very important to America's position in world affairs. We educate, the historically Black colleges and universities, a mass of young people who might not otherwise have an opportunity to get an education. It does not mean that they do not have the intellectual capacity of college-level work; often they lacked exposure, and they lacked the means of financing their education. And they come into an environment at an HBCU knowing that they are with people who really care and they are nurturing. It is a nurturing, supportive environment. They are not just a number. They have names and faces, and success is very important. (Mary Frances, personal communication, August 15, 2005)

I think I could be president at another kind of institution, but I do not think that my passion and commitment would be as great. I definitely have a passion for this university and a commitment to all historically Black colleges and universities. (Dr. Bobby Isaac, personal communication, July 12, 2005)

For me it meant going home to a home that I had never been to, but Afro American had always been my thing, and you do know that I am Black. I joke and tell folks I have been Black all my life; it's not something I just decided to become. The folks on the committee said, "You're going to an

HBCU . . . you've never been here." I said, "Well, wait a minute. I didn't decide just yesterday on this Black thing, I have been Black forever in every way [laughs]." As long as I can remember I have been Black is what I told folks, so it was a conscious decision because I really did believe that a lot of the values, a lot of my goals, I could make a difference here. I wanted to believe that I could make a difference everywhere I have been, but I decided that I could make an even greater difference here than I could at other schools. (Dr. Kerry Foster, personal communication, July 7, 2005)

Yes [it was conscious], because I started my life at what one would call a major institution. . . . As hard as I worked there, there was a social piece that was missing and having been the product of an HBCU, that is, Howard, where my whole life revolved around the university. . . . At this university I did my work and I separated and I was not socially or culturally in the tapestry of the institution. Since this was going to be my life's work, I made a conscious decision to find something that would give me peace to know that I was doing my work in an area where I was needed and appreciated, and where I as an individual would feel as if I had not sold out my race and so, yes, it was a conscious decision to find work at an HBCU and to let it be my life's work. In essence it is a cliché, but people say you bloom where you're planted. (Dr. Mathilda Marie, personal communication, July 29, 2005)

All of the presidents' responses indicate that leading a Black college or university provides them with a great sense of personal and professional gratification. They choose to work on these campuses because they want to give back and are committed to making a difference in the lives of African American youth. The presidents find great fulfillment in knowing their work is appreciated. Although numerous higher education institutions exist, the presidents believe that the need is greatest on Black college campuses. They feel connected to the institutions because many them attended Black colleges as undergraduates. This kinship ultimately forces them to take on the responsibility of making these schools better because in their opinion, Black colleges serve a critical function. The decision to lead them, therefore, is an easy one. Dr. Mathilda Marie said it best, "You bloom where you're planted" (personal communication, July 29, 2005).

The attitude toward choosing the presidency at a Black college was not completely positive for all of the study participants. Prior to assuming their positions, two presidents openly shared a few of their reservations about working at an HBCU:

I made some generalizations about HBCUs that were not necessarily positive at this time 25 years ago: autocratic leadership, poor financial management at the business office and at the financial aid office; a lot of nepotism, people being hired because of who they know, who they are related to rather than cause they have the skills necessary for the job. Academic programs that were good but not necessarily as good as they could be and people not seeming to care . . . I didn't think that it necessarily had to be that way so I was looking for an opportunity to demonstrate that things could be different at HBCUs, and that was basically what led me to HBCUs. (Dr. Sultan Rovaris, personal communication, August 15, 2005)

I had decided that to work at an HBCU I had to be able to come in at a level where I could really make some changes and make an impact. In particular from student affairs . . . a lot of the student affairs folks at HBCUs did not have the classic student affairs training; they sort of just ended up in it, but they didn't get a master's in student personnel. Most of them are counselors and don't have Ph.D.s in higher education. (Dr. Earl Davis, personal communication, August 2, 2005)

Despite their reservations, both presidents approached the decision to lead Black institutions from genuine concern. The negative perceptions did not distance them from Black campuses, but rather motivated them to want to have a positive impact and effect meaningful change. An interesting observation is that the two presidents who shared their skepticism did not attend or work in an HBCU environment. They graduated from and worked exclusively on predominantly White college campuses, yet absent direct engagement some of the presidents developed negative beliefs of Black colleges. The problem is that they made generalizations about this group of institutions, and this contributes to negative perceptions that plague Black colleges: they are regularly misunderstood and often misrepresented (Brown & Freeman, 2004; Fleming, 1984; Willie, 1994).

Dr. Kerry Foster shared a similar generalization when he discussed his decision to become president of an HBCU. He feared that Black colleges did not have the resources to compensate him adequately, so he considered other options. Dr. Foster admitted that he intended to work at a Black college, but only at the end of his career. This confession speaks volumes and raises critical concerns. Why is a waiting period necessary? African American students, professors, and administrators often attest to the benefits of attending HBCUs, but when they have an opportunity to work at these schools, they decide to wait. What are they waiting for? Surely money is a valid issue since Black colleges have struggled to compete with majority institutions. But if everyone waits, who will serve the students on these campuses? For Black colleges to continue to flourish, they must be equipped with a strong faculty and administration whose members are eager and choose not to wait.

## *The Influence of Family and Mentors*

In addition to their credentials and work experience, the presidents mentioned the importance of family and mentors and their influence on their path to the presidency. Family set expectations at an early age. The expectation was not to be a college president, per se, but that the key to a successful life is in a good education. They learned to appreciate the value of an education and recognized that, as African Americans, an education is an imperative tool. The educational background of the presidents' parents, in particular, was influential. Some of the presidents came from homes whose family members did not earn a high school diploma or a college degree. They, in turn, used this as a source of motivation to do better with the opportunities presented to them. Their parents' lack of education motivated them to want more education.

Similarly, presidents reared by college-educated families knew the expectation because their parents served as real models. They were fortunate enough to grow up experiencing the benefits of an education. Families not only exposed them to the value of higher education in general, but specifically to the value of HBCUs. According to Dr. Scales Donahoo:

> My father and mother were both graduates of TSU [Tennessee State University] and, in fact, that's where they met. They both earned their degrees from TSU and each worked for TSU for 39 years. So when my parents built a home, they literally built a home facing the men's dormitory. I basically grew up across the street from TSU. The first couple of years of my life, I lived in an apartment above the health center at TSU. My family goes way back with TSU. (personal communication, July 7, 2005)

This recollection is indicative of many of the presidents' experiences. The exposure to HBCUs through their parents allowed them the opportunity to establish a certain level of comfort and familiarity with the institutions. In the case of Dr. Scales Donahoo, he followed in his parents' footsteps and attended Tennessee State University as an undergraduate. Dr.

Earl Davis, on the other hand, attended predominantly White institutions but marveled at his parents' accomplishment of graduating from two HBCUs. Although he did not have the connection firsthand, the stories his parents shared provided him with a glimpse of the Black college experience.

While family influenced presidents by setting the expectation to get an education, mentors played a critical role in guiding their careers toward the college presidency. Eighty percent of the study participants reported that the presidency was not a calculated career move, so, somewhere along their journey, someone planted a new seed of expectation. Dr. Clarence Myers, for example, said that his mentor, a college president, told him he had presidential potential, and this sparked his interest in pursuing the position. Dr. Scales Donahoo had not heard of Philander Smith College when his mentor asked him if he would be interested in the presidency. His mentor encouraged him and took the liberty of nominating him for his first presidential appointment. After Dr. Donahoo served as president for a few years, his mentor nominated him again, this time for the presidency at Jemison State University. Overall, mentors played a significant role in encouraging the presidents to think beyond the limits they set for themselves.

# 4

# MISSION MATTERS AT HISTORICALLY BLACK INSTITUTIONS

Brown (2003) identifies several fallacies associated with research on historically Black colleges and universities (HBCUs). He argues that the fallacy of assumptive evidence occurs when researchers make assumptions about Black colleges based on earlier nonempirical scholarship. This process ignites a vicious cycle, perpetuating false representations of Black colleges that are rooted primarily in unsubstantiated information. The findings of this study, however, are a result of systematic investigation and credible participation. Through semistructured interviews, 15 presidents shared their perspectives on the topic of mission based on their experiences as leaders of Black colleges. The findings are significant because they provide a fresh view on an abandoned topic first broached by W.E.B. Du Bois and Booker T. Washington while serving as a building block for future research.

What is the mission of HBCUs? Mission refers to the explicit role, purpose, and function of the institution. This question forces presidents to reflect on their schools' distinct place within the larger academy and ultimately to ask, "What is our reason for being?" The conceptual framework of the study proposes that raising this rather broad question allows presidents the opportunity to engage in what Weick (1995) identifies as sensemaking. The process of sensemaking is concerned with ways in which individuals construct meaning and generate interpretations. Sensemaking is valuable, particularly for defining the mission of HBCUs, because things that are easily taken for granted are not questioned. Sensemaking calls for everyday things, everyday assumptions, to be questioned.

The research question is, "How do presidents of four-year, historically Black colleges and universities define the mission of their institutions?" It attempts to gain varying perspectives on mission, recognizing the diversity that exists among HBCUs. According to Brown (2003):

> The idea that mission adoption and adherence are universal and consistent across and throughout all Black colleges is the fallacy of mission stability. There is not a cogent mission statement that can be universally applied to all Black colleges. Moreover, if there were, there would not be and is not consistent application of that mission across all Black colleges. Research that attempts to investigate whether Black colleges are fulfilling their mission is deceived by the assumption of mission stability. No cohort of institutions is the same perennially in an omnipresent and circumstantial form. The way in which institutions individually and even collectively define their mission is contingent on time, place, and circumstance. (p. 38)

This book adheres to Brown's (2003) assertion and does not seek to produce a solitary definition of mission applicable to all HBCUs, but rather to create a more comprehensive view drawn from multiple perspectives. The intent is to allow four-year presidents from different backgrounds who are leaders of various types of Black colleges to share their personal definitions of their institution's mission. Do their perspectives collide or coincide?

## Common Themes

Despite the diversity of the sample of HBCUs represented in this book, the presidents shared similar perspectives toward defining the mission of their schools. To convey their responses, the research uses theme analysis, which refers to recurring qualities or characteristics that provide explanation to research inquiry (McMillan & Schumacher, 1997). Based on the interview responses, the presidents shared the following common themes with regard to defining mission: access and opportunity, preparation for leadership, and land-grant mission.

### *Access and Opportunity*

In defining the mission of their respective institutions, the presidents' most consistent response was that HBCUs provide African Americans with access and opportunity. Black colleges developed during a time dominated by legal segregation and racial discrimination and out of necessity because predominantly White schools would not admit African Americans students. Although Black students are currently free to apply to colleges and universities throughout the nation, the presidents' declare that the mission of Black colleges is to remain committed to serving the African American students by providing them with more educational options. The following responses illustrate how presidents define the mission of their historically Black higher education institution:

> I think that the purpose is to give people the opportunity to reach their academic potential. This school, as is the case with most HBCUs, believes strongly in people having opportunities and not being highly selective in terms of eliminating the opportunities before a person can have a chance to go to their first class . . . hopefully their potential is to successfully complete a baccalaureate program. (Dr. Scales Donahoo, personal communication, July 7, 2005)

> There are a couple of words that I think clearly define the mission of this university. The mission really is to deal with access, opportunity, and affordability; to be sure that we are providing opportunities for that segment of the population that might be underserved or is underserved and would not necessarily be served by other institutions within society. (Dr. Bobby Isaac, personal communication, July 12, 2005)

> Well, I think that the mission of [Giovanni State University] is that it continues to have a commitment to providing opportunities for students of African decent that are not available on many other campuses. Secondly, [Giovanni State University] is [a] state institution, so part of its mission is to be available to students in the state regardless of background. (Dr. Sultan Rovaris, personal communication, August 15, 2005)

> It is an educational institution designated as primarily serving students for baccalaureate education, with some selected associate degree programs, that is designed primarily to offer an affordable education to students in the state and other places in the world as well, including foreign students as well as persons from other states, but primarily a baccalaureate institution. (Dr. Lyelle Boutte, personal communication, September 26, 2005)

> The dominant reason this institution was founded was to educate people of color; that was the dominant reason, and so my major mission is to

bring education to people of color. I am a comprehensive university doing what comprehensive universities do. I offer the bachelor's, master's, and doctoral degrees so scholarship inquiry engagement, all of that student learning, all of those factors come into the mission of providing comprehensive education. (Dr. Mathilda Marie, personal communication, July 29, 2005)

Well, succinctly for us, it really has been to provide that access to higher education for academically talented students and those who have the potential to be talented. . . . We are not unlike most HBCUs. There are a few elite institutions that have not had to address these issues, but the vast majority are in the situation like us. Simply put, after *Brown v. Board*, 90% of Black folks who went to college went to HBCUs. After that happened it was a whole new ball game, White institutions got in the game for Black students and really have just out-competed Black schools, and so now 16% of all Black students attend HBCUs. So schools are just staying open really by just admitting whoever they can. . . . So you have the most at-risk students that are coming in with marginal GPAs, some less than 2.0., marginal standardized test scores, and poor family background. So we're just struggling along trying to keep doors open because the game has changed a lot, and unfortunately I think that they [HBCUs] were really slower to react to that. And so I grew up in Atlanta with all those HBCUs there, I was number two in my class, and there was no HBCU in Atlanta that actively recruited me, and that is ridiculous. It's sort of like, I keep trying to tell people, I have to tell the president at Morehouse they need to give me an honorary degree because every time I tell people I'm from Atlanta, they assume I went to Morehouse. I'm like, "No I went to Georgia, Morehouse never recruited me." And so this is mid-'80s. We didn't go after the top kids nationally. And now people are scrambling because it is like, whoa, we are having trouble making our budgets and numbers are dropping and schools are closing. All that is happening, and so people keep the doors open basically. Like I challenge our institution, it's not so much the academically talented because we're getting few of those students. We are getting those that have potential, and now potential sometimes is just defined as those who are living and breathing and not in terms of any proven academic potential. It's just like they have an interest in coming to college and we admit those students. (Dr. Earl Davis, personal communication, August 2, 2005)

The presidents in the study assert that the mission of HBCUs is to serve students with varying needs by providing access and opportunity. Many students, particularly African American students, who enter college are not academically prepared due to poor schooling at the elementary, middle, and high school levels. The presidents contend that Black colleges give these students the opportunity to pursue higher education because the focus is on their potential.

Dr. Earl Davis, the youngest and newest president, was noticeably the most critical of those sampled, but he provided thoughtful insight into defining the mission. He argued that Black colleges do a poor job of recruiting high-caliber African American students. Surely, most majority institutions have more resources and incentives to offer, but Dr. Davis contends that Black colleges do not even attempt to compete. This lack of effort contributes to the enrollment of African American students at predominantly White colleges and universities, as high-achieving students are overlooked. A challenge for Black colleges, therefore, is accepting the consequences of not recruiting top scholars. Dr. Davis offers that Black colleges must recognize and embrace their mission of educating students who lack proper academic preparation.

Historically Black colleges and universities have the special ability to meet students wherever they are and transform them into successful college graduates. While Black colleges vary in their admissions policies, many accept students with low grade point averages and meager standardized test scores. The overwhelming response of the sample, however, was that the access and opportunities Black colleges provide, particularly for African American students, remain unparalleled in majority colleges and universities. In comparison to most predominantly White institutions, Black colleges tend to have lower tuition rates, which makes pursuing higher education there a more attainable goal.

Historically Black colleges and universities are an option among the many higher education institutions available to high school graduates. Predominantly White institutions no longer prohibit African American student participation, so Black students are free to enroll in these schools. Students attend the schools of their choice, and the presidents recognized that all Black students do not have to attend an HBCU. Dr. Kerry Foster stated:

I tell people, and maybe you'll say I'm overstating it, if you are admitted to UT [University of Texas] Austin and you don't go to UT Austin, there are a lot of other good schools you could go to. If you're admitted to Duke and you don't go to Duke, where do you go? Vanderbilt, Emory, U.Va. [University of Virginia], Princeton, my heavens, those are pretty good options. For many students, if you don't go to [Shabazz University] you don't go to college, and that's a big difference. (personal communication, August 12, 2005)

This argument reflects the harsh reality that many African American students do not have options in their quest to attain a college degree. History reveals that African Americans struggled merely to gain the right to an education, and early on their education was separate and unequal. As a result, the schooling process left lasting deficiencies that continue to affect their ability to succeed and place them at a considerable disadvantage. Black colleges, for some Black students, are their saving grace as these schools recognize that a deficiency does not mean defeat. Students are able to pursue their dream of a higher education, which otherwise might not have been possible. The consensus among the presidents in the study is that Black colleges serve a necessary mission. Dr. Clarence Myers summed it up best by saying that, although students can attend many colleges and universities, "HBCUs are the best shot at getting African American students through" (personal communication, July 7, 2005).

### Preparation for Leadership

In addition to providing access and opportunity, a common theme among the presidents was that the mission of HBCUs is to prepare students for leadership roles. Kannerstein (1978) identified leadership as a critical component of the mission of Black colleges, and the following interview responses reveal how the presidents value leadership:

We have a liberal arts perspective, and we educate men and women for leadership, for citizenship, to use their education to make a difference and to affect change, certainly in a global world today. But that has been part of [Winfrey College's] mission . . . we have always been able to produce those young people who go out into the world and use their education to uplift humanity. (Mary Frances, personal communication, August 15, 2005)

I would say that [Chisholm's] mission is, in its uniqueness, buried in the the experience of historically Black colleges over the past almost 200 years. Historically Black colleges in this country have been a principal route for African Americans in particular to gain access to higher education and then to have a developmental experience that has prepared a distinct majority of African Americans for leadership and for professional pursuits in our country that would not have otherwise happened. (Devon Lamard, personal communication, August 15, 2005)

If you go back to the historical mission of [Height University] . . . the mission was to create a leadership class for the African American community and that is still part of the fabric of this institution. We want to produce a leadership class for the globe. . . . So that is what we want to do . . . create these pathways to leadership positions for our students so that they can operate in a diverse and global environment. (Dr. John Spencer, personal communication, August 19, 2005)

I would describe the university as one that is student centered. We do perceive our students as our customers and as such, everything that we do, we ultimately want it to enhance and enrich the lives of students who enroll and come to us. We prepare our students when they graduate to be able to go to the world from [Walker University] . . . when they believe that they are prepared to go to the world and become leaders, that sets a higher standard. Many students come, and all they know is their community. They can go back to their communities, that's alright; they are prepared to go to any community, not only in America, but in the world. (Dr. Trevis Freeman, personal communication, July 7, 2005)

Our primary purpose is really to create the kinds of educational experiences that enable particularly minority citizens to gain some distinct advantages, position themselves for leadership, and position themselves into the world and become part of that cadre that not only by their very action change the world, but that they also impact in a conscious way the structure and nature of things. So we talk about gaining distinct economic advantage, we talk about imbuing our students with a definitive sense of public service, we believe in servant leadership; we preach and teach it all the time, but also positioning themselves for leadership in all things (Dr. Jared Auguste, personal communication, July 20, 2005)

Presidents of Black colleges promote the notion that the mission of their schools is to equip students with the necessary tools to consciously take on positions of leadership. The goal is for students to take what they have learned on Black college campuses and use their knowledge and skills to make positive change in both the African American community and the world at large. The objective is to teach them to think beyond the confines of their respective environments and make a difference globally.

The mission of Black colleges is to instill a sense of responsibility in their students to serve others, to give back and make meaningful contributions to the world. Presidents value leadership because it serves as an avenue for African Americans to acquire positions of power and influence. Historically Black colleges and universities remain the undergraduate home of the majority of African American leaders in this country (Brown, 2002b; Browning & Williams, 1978; Fleming, 1984; Garibaldi, 1984; Roebuck & Murty, 1993). The presidents in the research study, therefore, aspire to continue this legacy.

### Land-Grant Mission

Forty percent of the HBCUs represented in the study were land-grant institutions, colleges or universities designated by Congress to receive funds to educate students in agriculture, mechanical arts, and military training as a result of the Morrill Act of 1862 and the Morrill Act of 1890 (Brown, 1999; Cohen, 1998; Geiger, 1999). When asked to define the mission of their college or university, 50% of the presidents of land-grant schools mentioned their land-grant mission. Dr. Mathilda Marie, president of University of Angelou, stated, "Our institution is a land-grant institution, which means we have a special charge to look at conserving the environment, the ocean around us, the air, and the land" (personal communication, July 29, 2005).

Walker University president, Dr. Trevis Freeman, echoed the sentiment:

[Walker University] is the state's only historically African American university. It is classified as an 1890 land-grant institution. . . . Our mission is a very unique mission in that we, as a land-grant institution, have the responsibility, as all land-grant universities have, for research, teaching, outreach, and community service; that's the overall focus of our institution. In research, our focus as a land-grant institution has been on a niche in the animal kingdom that we decided to focus our agriculture focus on and that, of course, is the goat. We are and have developed at [Walker University] the world's largest center for goat research. We are it, and those goats have taken us to the world. We provide research as well as train scientists in goat research in all aspects that include nutrition, meat, fiber, the cashmere goats. We raise goats and help the government use them in conservation in the mountains. We use our goats to assist the Bureau of Land Management as well as other forest services of the United States in controlling the undergrowth in parts of America. So we are goat research; we are the goat ropers of the country. (Dr. Trevis Freeman, personal communication, July 7, 2005)

The presidents' recognition of their land-grant mission indicates that their institutions remain committed to fulfilling their responsibilities as dictated by the Morrill acts. The presidents, however, did not limit their schools' mission solely to land-grant duties. They emphasized the importance of providing their students with a wide range of educational pursuits by exposing them to myriad academic majors. None of the presidents of land-grant institutions, however, mentioned their land-grant mission. This omission was a surprise considering the amount of financial support given to these schools because of their status as land-grant colleges and universities. Perhaps the presidents simply neglected to mention this function, or maybe the land-grant mission is not an integral part of their campuses.

## Divergent Perspectives

In addition to the common defining themes of access and opportunity, preparation for leadership, and the land-grant function, the presidents in the study offered divergent perspectives when asked to define the mission of their respective HBCU. These perspectives merit recognition because they broaden the idea of what constitutes the mission of Black colleges. Mission is a comprehensive term, and the presidents' responses encompassed many dimensions as a result of the diverse nature of the historically Black schools they lead.

According to Dr. Nathan Dudley, "The mission of [Tubman University] is to train Christian leaders to lead the church and the global community" (personal communication, July 20, 2005). Tubman serves a more specialized function than the other HBCUs represented in the study because it is a Christian graduate school of theology. Its identity as a school of theology dictates that its mission is dedicated to educating young men and women in preparation for the ministry. Tubman's mission incorporates the common theme of preparing students for leadership; however, the leadership at this particular institution concentrates on helping students become spiritual leaders as teachers, pastors, and preachers.

Walker University president Dr. Trevis Freeman revealed that a critical component of his institution's mission is an ongoing commitment to providing international programs and opportunities for their student body:

> As an African American university, we believe it is important to give students an opportunity to learn more about Africa particularly, and other countries. So our study abroad program is six weeks where students go and get six hour credits in various parts of Africa: South Africa, West Africa, down in the Caribbean, Dominican Republic, and, this year, Belize and many of the underdeveloped countries in the world. We are finding that the experience broadens their perspectives of themselves, of the world, and they benefit much. We have a strong international program here. We've created a degree in international studies where the students learn the critical languages. Now that we live in a world community, and because of the diversity of our campus, we have access on the campus. A lot of people can teach a lot of these languages such as Japanese and Chinese. Historically, all we've ever been able to do is French, German, and Spanish, but the critical languages now are these others, so we now offer those in addition to the basics. We have a degree in teaching English as a second language and that's one of our master's programs because, with our urban mission in preparing our teachers to go into the urban centers of America particularly, they have to be diverse and be able to teach English as a second language, which is becoming more and more important. (personal communication, July 7, 2005)

This view of mission illustrates this president's concern for exposing students to the international world. The focus on Africa, in particular, suggests that the school values the idea of educating African American students about their ancestry. The study abroad programs allow students to see the world and fully experience life and culture outside the United States. This mission of international exposure recognizes the increased need for students at HBCUs to be equipped with an awareness and understanding of the global world to be viable candidates for the competitive job market.

## Implementing the Mission

Defining the mission of HBCUs involves articulating the overall purpose, role, and function of these institutions. The articulation, however, is only the first step. The next phase of the study shifts the focus from the colleges and universities to the role of the president. The guiding research question is, "How do presidents of historically Black colleges and universities implement the mission of their institutions?" The objective is to understand how the presidents make mission manifest. How do they contribute to carrying out the mission they articulate?

## Common Themes

The president plays a vital role in ensuring that the college or university is functioning properly (Birnbaum, 1988b; Buchanan, 1988). Maintenance and supervision responsibilities, coupled with the pressures and expectations of leading an academic institution, distinctly separates the position of president from other higher education administrators (Birnbaum, 1992; Cohen & March, 1986; Kauffman, 1980). The presidents in the study shared two common themes that identified their role in implementing the mission of their respective college or university. The first is that the presidents view themselves as visible representatives of their institutions, and the second is that they use strategic planning to accomplish the mission they articulate.

### The Representative of the School

Representative is an inclusive term that identifies the president as an authoritative presence on campus. As representatives, presidents have certain responsibilities, and with those responsibilities come expectations. They are expected to be involved with campus matters and decision making because they represent the voice of their institutions. As the representatives, the presidents possess power and influence. The following interview responses demonstrate how the presidents in the study, as representatives of their schools, described their role in implementing the mission of their HBCUs:

> The president serves as the face on this mission, providing the motivation, focusing all of the attention on being sure that this vision and this mission is accomplished, and being certain and accountable to the board and other stakeholders for the fulfillment of that mission. The president has to be sure that the resources of the university are aligned with the mission and its strategic plans and aims. That is the role of the president, and that is easier said than done. (Dr. Bobby Isaac, personal communication, July 12, 2005)

Everything runs through this office because they want my input. In this state, the institutions are known by the president and what the president does. Presidents set the tone and adhere to the mission. As the president you have to recognize the need and find the resources to grow and prosper. (Dr. Clarence Myers, personal communication, July 7, 2005)

A president helps to define an institution's character and ethos in part by how he interacts with that community and how he positions himself within that community and how he models what the institution is all about. (Dr. Jared Auguste, personal communication, July 20, 2005)

I play a role in implementing the mission at all levels. I am engaged in the faculty meetings, directing the activities of my vice presidents and people who directly report to me play a role. As the chief spokesman for the institution and as the principal fund-raiser for the institution, I have a critical role in fulfilling the mission of the institution. (Dr. Nathan Dudley, personal communication, July 20, 2005)

I think that the president is that person who tries to make the mission statement come to life, which is why we're looking at ours and probably by the time I get out of here, it will change because it needs to be something that is succinct enough. Most mission statements are too long and too elaborate [so] that people don't know what they mean anyway. So we have got to condense it to something that everybody around campus can grasp, and everybody can speak the sentence that this is what we are about, and then we do all these different things to make this happen. So part of it will be to be that spokesperson for . . . but right now we're going through a phase where I'm really trying to help us redefine what the mission is so that we're all the same page to say this is our mission. (Dr. Earl Davis, personal communication, August 2, 2005)

The president is the voice. You have to step up to the plate. You cannot lead from behind. Your institution, fortunately or unfortunately, you represent it. When you speak, people see [Walker University] and must hear [Walker University], and that's kind of how I have maneuvered. I do believe in shared purposes. I do share a lot of responsibilities. I have strong teams including students in the process. I believe that my style has been that of engagement on the part of the entire university. All of our publics must buy in to the success of the university. (Dr. Trevis Freeman, personal communication, July 7, 2005)

The presidents' responses identify a few of the key roles and responsibilities of the Black college presidency. As the highest-ranking chief academic officers, they serve a critical function as representatives of their colleges and universities. Presidents confront accountability issues and have to ensure that their schools are providing the services they promote and meeting the needs of the campus and community. They are the face of their colleges and universities and ultimately have the task of setting the tone of the overall campus. It is interesting to note that the mere mention of a president's name is synonymous with his or her institution. Consequently, the reputations of Black college presidents influence the perception of their schools.

The expectation is that presidents, as institutional leaders, will take charge and implement the mission of their college and university in the appropriate manner. But to implement mission, presidents need adequate resources. While they have countless responsibilities, a significant part of their job includes fund-raising. Fund-raising is an important responsibility, particularly for presidents of HBCUs, due to the financial constraints these institutions endure. Resources allow presidents the opportunity to turn their institutions' missions into reality. Without resources, presidents cannot initiate new academic programs, recruit new faculty, or renovate aging facilities. The challenge, therefore, is finding innovative ways to acquire the necessary funds so the mission may be carried out.

Although the president is the representative of the school and has to stay abreast of all university operations, he or she recognizes that mission implementation does not occur in isolation. Indeed, presidents have power, but their success as leaders and the prosperity of their schools is contingent on the support and involvement of faculty, staff, students, and the community. The effort is a collective one, and to implement mission, presidents must have a strategic plan.

*Strategic Planning*

Presidents, as representatives of colleges and universities, define mission and seek the resources to implement that mission, and the next logical phase involves strategic planning. Higher education is a major enterprise. Colleges and universities are organized in a hierarchical manner composed of many individuals. Despite their elaborate hierarchy of power and command, for institutions to reach maximum potential, all invested individuals must work hard and demonstrate dedication to accomplish the established mission.

Presidents of HBCUs acknowledge that they do not work alone and that it takes a whole village to implement the missions of their respective schools. Three of the presidents participating in the study offered the following perspectives:

> When I came here in 1987, we started a strategic planning process. We have a record of having three-year strategic plans. The strategic plans are divided among the administrative divisions. There's a plan for academic affairs, planning and advancement, administration, finance, and student affairs. And each plan is a three-year plan, and we have three-year goals with annual objectives and quarterly strategies, and that is the format for the plan. The goals and objectives are related to the mission statement. The strategic plan for each division is driven by the mission statement. In every quarter I would meet with each vice president to find out how they are doing in terms of the strategies for their plans, and now I do that on a monthly basis. And that is how I'm able to monitor how we're doing in terms of making certain that our priorities are consistent with our mission statement. We're now in our sixth cycle of strategic planning. (Dr. Scales Donahoo, personal communication, July 7, 2005)

> I am the leader of the institution, and the buck stops here. I believe in strategic planning, and I believe in the implementation of the strategic plan so that your strategic plan grows out from your mission. So you look at your mission statement and you look at what the state requires of you and you formulate your strategic initiative to match that. When I finish my strategic plan, everybody who works at the institution must see themselves in it. It's like a family portrait. If your family took a portrait, and you didn't see yourself in it, something is wrong with the portrait. So, whether you cut the grass or teach graduate students or undergraduates, which is so important, or greet people on the telephone or work in security, you are to be effective in this strategic plan, which is geared toward improving the institution and working towards learning outcomes, and I keep telling them, making good better. . . . My role is to make sure that it is implemented, and it's not just a document that you do and it's good and you put it on the shelf. We have periodic meetings to see how we are accomplishing our goals, and then you have an assessment plan that's tied into it and you do your research to make sure that what you say you would like to do, you've done, and then you take the results and work it into the new plan for next year. And so we have a five-year plan, but we also have an

annual plan to see what we've accomplished, and then I do an annual report, which is very much an overview, it's not a detailed report. But the president's role in all of this for me, because we are a small university with only just about 4,000 students right now. . . . The president wears many hats. I am hands-on. I sit at the table and write things and answer my own mail and do things; I'm not just a figurehead president going about talking about what other people do. I write proposals and get them funded. I am literally a part of the workforce, not just the leader. If I do this, my vice president also must do this and everyone involved is to be a productive contributing citizen. My job is to make sure that is true. (Dr. Mathilda Marie, personal communication, July 29, 2005)

One is the development and communication and inculcation of a vision derived from the mission derived from history derived from the character and culture of the institution. But that projects it forward in ways that perhaps others can't immediately see; not only about the future of the institution but the future of the people that are here. So articulating communication and inculcating vision is one thing that I have to do. . . . The second thing is that one must be very conscious of definitive, practical, strategic planning, which is how do you get to the vision? How do you use the mission to structure a root to the vision? That is the process by which you enable the community, the university community itself, to design its various paths to that vision and to take ownership of those paths and to hold themselves and each other accountable for the annual pursuit of that vision. (Dr. Jared Auguste, personal communication, July 20, 2005)

The interview responses illustrate the presidents' engagement in symbolic interactionism, a social psychological theory that suggests that people make meanings through social interactions (Bogdan & Biklen, 1998). The presidents in this study define and implement mission based on the consideration and involvement of others.

Strategic planning helps presidents of HBCUs get organized in preparation for mission implementation. The presidents establish a reasonable time frame to get the work accomplished. Although time frames vary from one institution to the next, the overall objective is to get everyone, including the faculty, students, administration, and the surrounding community, to work toward common goals. The president's job is to create a campus of shared responsibility and strategically develop teams to achieve the mission of the institution. Teams allow individuals an opportunity to play an active role in the planning process and provide a platform for their voices to be heard and incorporated into the agenda. Dr. Mathilda Marie, a female president, offered an interesting perspective with regard to involving the entire campus community in the strategic planning process. She said that at Winfrey College, her strategic plan is like a family portrait. Dr. Marie's goal is to ensure that everyone who attends and works at the institution sees him- or herself in the portrait. The family portrait strategic plan idea is an excellent way to encourage shared responsibility and campus involvement.

The presidents in the study stressed the importance of the history of Black colleges and universities. Despite the progress of these institutions, the presidents remain mindful of the struggle and the historic mission of educating African American students. The presidents relied heavily on the mission statements adopted by their colleges and universities, which serve as the foundation on which many of the presidents build their strategic plans.

## Complementary Perspectives

The following perspectives offered by presidents in the study echo the common themes of being a representative of the school and strategic planning. The responses, however, add new dimensions to the way in which the implementation process occurs.

> Generally my role in almost everything that goes on at the university is to make sure that I put into place the best-qualified individuals in leadership roles and then provide the resources, human and material, for them to do their jobs the best that they could. So when we speak about the land-grant mission, for example, we had a highly qualified dean of our college of agriculture, and I worked with him regularly and directly, and through the vice president for academic affairs, to ensure that he had the resources necessary to move that college forward and to bring the university's land-grant mission forward. And the same is true with regard to the commitment to African American students since this school's inception in 1895. Our associate vice president for enrollment management . . . his responsibility was to ensure that the doors were open for African American students where possible, and we admitted those students and ensured that they were retained to the best of our ability and ultimately graduate. (Dr. Sultan Rovaris, personal communication, August 15, 2005)

> As the president of the college, we establish a vision for the institution that is built upon the consensus and input from the members of the institution.

I draw from the history of this great college, and I look at where we are today, where we want to be in the future. I look at the whole context of higher education and how the landscape is changing and where do we want [Winfrey College] to fit in. I put faces and words to that mission, particularly that I am able to communicate that, work to get not only the college community here to buy in, but also our external constituents—alumni, friends, donors, to look at [Winfrey College] and to promote that every day to bring the vision of the college before the members of the [Winfrey College] community and also for our alumni and friends through communication, with face-to-face meetings, through expressions in the written form and in the spoken form. (Mary Frances, personal communication, August 15, 2005)

I am responsible to ensure that every aspect of that mission is accomplished. We place students first and everything that we do is geared toward successful student performance. In order to achieve successful student performance . . . that means graduation, and graduation with the qualifications to go on to a higher level, to postgraduate-level education, and to enter professional fields. . . . Then you must develop and maintain relevant academic programs that meet the needs of students. You must take a larger view towards student development that's not only the classroom, but it's outside of the classroom in terms of their cultural, moral, holistic development so that students not only understand their academic courses. They have to develop academically, but they also need to develop in a holistic way so that they are able to perform well within the rigors of society that will ask them to do a lot of other things other than just performing their profession. Secondly, we must have the facilities, the infrastructure, and the overall environment for students that enhance learning and that takes care of them well . . . that provides them a good surrounding to study and for living and for social development as well. We have a responsibility to maintain our attachment to the past and building roads to the future, and that's through our alumni and through other associations and relationships that help to propel the university forward on a continuing basis. Our university has a responsibility for being a good citizen and espousing good citizenship in the surrounding communities and in the area in which we live. Then we also must capitalize and develop our human capital, that human capital being faculty, being staff . . . because we can only continue to put students first as we enrich our human capital and make certain that we have the right people in the right jobs providing the right things for our students. (Devon Lamard, personal communication, August 16, 2005)

Well, obviously, the decisions I make from a day-to-day basis should be guided by the mission because, after all, if you don't look at that mission, then you take the university outside of what it is intended to do. My decisions, my involvement in the community, my involvement in the state, my involvement outside the state all was geared toward making sure that Black citizens had the opportunity to get a higher education. (Dr. Acosta Lee, personal communication, August 25, 2005)

First of all . . . I tell my faculty this all the time and I really mean it; when you really look at the mission of a university, that mission is delivered in large part by the faculty. So how I implement that mission here at the institution is that I am engaged in the recruitment of faculty, in the retention of faculty, and in their professional development. I also play an active role in the recruitment of students to the university, and so I am very concerned about the recruitment and retention of students and creating ways for them to go on to graduate and professional school; especially to get Ph.D.s and plant that seed that, once they get the Ph.D., that they will come back to their alma mater and be a part of this faculty and administration. (Dr. John Spencer, personal communication, August 19, 2005)

To implement the mission of their HBCUs successfully, presidents surround themselves with individuals who contribute to helping the mission manifest itself. The object is to employ qualified people for key leadership and faculty positions. The presidents' jobs become easier when they can rely on and share responsibilities with a competent group of administrators and faculty. As previously mentioned, mission implementation does not occur in isolation. In addition to appreciating the input of students and faculty, the presidents expressed a desire to have more participation from alumni and donors. The relationships with alumni and donors aid in the growth of Black colleges because they contribute to the financial well-being of the institutions. The challenge for Black colleges is finding ways to nurture those relationships and establish meaningful connections. The goal is to encourage alumni and donors to get involved with the campus so they are able to contribute to the needs of the school.

## Challenges to Mission Implementation

The presidents in the study play a key role in defining and implementing the mission of Black colleges. While they are able to easily set the parameters of what their institutions are expected to do and establish their particular role in aiding the process, challenges often preclude them from reaching their desired goals. Black colleges have a long history of struggle as they developed during a time of intense racial segregation and discrimination. Although they have experienced growth and much success, Black colleges continue to face obstacles as they attempt to remain relevant institutions of higher education. This section of the book addresses the challenges presidents face when they attempt to implement the mission of their institutions. Despite the differences among HBCUs, they share similar struggles. The presidents in the study elaborated on the two common themes of financial constraints and resistance to change.

## Financial Constraints

Consistent with the literature on Black colleges, the dominant challenge these institutions endure is not having adequate financial resources (Allen & Jewell, 2002; Brown, Ricard, & Donahoo, 2004; Browning & Williams, 1978; Fleming 1984; Garibaldi, 1984; Kannerstein, 1978; Thompson, 1998). Colleges and universities are a business, and for any type of business to operate efficiently and reach its maximum potential, money is an absolute necessity. The problem, as evidenced in the following responses, is that money is such a powerful tool that it affects every aspect of a college or university's functioning.

> One of the primary barriers to all historically Black colleges and universities is the absence of discretionary funding. Most of the funds raised by and donated to historically Black colleges and universities tend to go to mission . . . there is an absence of discretionary funding to do some of the creative programming that we would like to do. So we must engage in writing a number of proposals and seeking external funding. (Dr. Nathan Dudley, personal communication, July 20, 2005)

> Certainly money is one [problem]. HBCUs do not receive the kind of support, be it foundation or personal from alumni, that predominantly White institutions receive. We typically don't have the same kinds of endowments. Secondly, as a public HBCU, we suffer from the fact that the board of regents and the chancellor's office still do not fully understand the function of historically Black colleges and universities so they don't receive the

kind of support that they should receive. (Dr. Sultan Rovaris, personal communication, August 15, 2005)

Well, the barriers that most institutions face today, even smaller institutions, particularly HBCUs, is funding and having adequate finances; the resources to really implement your vision and to do the kinds of things that you would really like to see done at your institutions. We have to find the available resources to help support the young people who are coming into our colleges who want an education. (Ms. Mary Frances, personal communication, August 15, 2005)

Since we are a state university, we are faced with the prospect of requiring more and more in terms of funding from individual students and their families. As we develop programs and infrastructure more and more for our universities today, we are expected to raise more and more of those dollars from outside sources. A lot of your success in fund-raising depends on your success with a number of other things that your university will have the capability to do. You also have to be concerned about a number of students that arrive at your university these days that are not exceptionally well prepared out of high school. You find yourself presented with the formidable challenge to bring your students along, and a number of them have a lot of catching up to do so you have to be concerned about that, and that gives you some barriers if you will. (Mr. Devon Lamard, personal communication August 16, 2005)

The challenge is that it is going to cost money to do things. Consequently, we have got to have the resources for them, and we also have to have the type of faculty, facilities, and so forth. We can't say to them [students], "come here," and then they've been on another campus and say, "Oh, yeah, we don't have those kinds of things because you know we're a Black school. We don't have the best lab . . ." They don't want to hear that stuff. They don't deserve that stuff. They deserve the best that other schools have. What it has meant, and people haven't liked it, we've had to raise the cost of attending this school substantially since I have been here. But before I ever came I said there are some good universities and there are some cheap universities. There are no good cheap universities. We are talking about an investment and so that is something else we have to do. The bottom line though, the biggest challenge would be our lack of will in making these things happen. Everywhere I've ever been all my life boils down to understanding there are barriers, roadblocks, and so forth. What are we going to do about it? How do we get to our goals anyway? The bottom line is, are we going to come up with a strategy to reach the goals that we set. I don't worry about these other things in the way because it's what I'm going to do, and that's been my whole story. (Dr. Kerry Foster, personal communication, August 12, 2005)

The biggest challenge is financial. Historically Black colleges and universities have been, are, and for some foreseeable future will be, underfunded. It makes it very difficult to do our job, so we have to do more with less and that's an awfully difficult task. But you know what, we've been doing it now for over a hundred years. We continue to do it and we do it very well. Other schools try, but they simply don't have that mentoring and nurturing atmosphere that we have at our HBCUs. (Dr. Acosta Lee, personal communication, August 25, 2005)

I think that the challenge to not just [Height University] but to almost all HBCUs has to do with funding. Funding takes on a lot of subcategories but, to give you an example, here in this state we have what you could pretty much call a tier system. Institutions are classified by their missions, and the way that you are classified impacts the salaries that can be paid to administrators as well as faculty. In this competitive marketplace that we have, if we're not able to get funding to pay competitive salaries, sometimes we miss out on the best talent and we have to make due with who we can recruit. The other part of the funding has to do with external fund-raising, not just from the state, but the ability to bring major gifts to institutions. You're studying higher education and what you're going to learn more and more as you go forward is that a lot of the fund-raising is dependent upon the types of programs that you have. In other words, corporations, for instance, want to invest in programs that will produce people who will eventually come and work for them. Well, if HBCUs don't have the programs, or the programs at the level that will attract the funding, then we continue to be in a position of struggle. So funding is one area, and I think another area is our facilities, our physical plant. More and more young people want to study in environments that are attractive, that are comfortable and have all of the things that you would expect in the 21st century. Because of this historical underinvestment in our institutions, some of our physical plants are not up to par. When young people and their families visit campuses and they want to go and see the dormitories, they want to see the library, they want to see the cafeteria, well if those facilities are not where they should be, our institutions are never going to be flagship institutions. Then

I think the other thing is enrollment. One of the things that defines the quality of an institution is the caliber of its student body, and we have to be, and when I see "we," I mean the HBCU community, needs to be in a position where we have a good chance of recruiting to our campuses the top talent, including National Achievement Scholars, National Merit Scholars, National Hispanic Scholars. Until we get a critical mass of students like that, then as these rankings come out, like *US News and World Report* and all these others, our institutions are not going to be there in significant numbers because much of what they use for these rankings have to do with graduation rates and retention rates. (Dr. John Spencer, personal communication, August 19, 2005)

I think that you will hear from almost every president that you will interview that the major challenge is funding. That is one of the major things all of us, not only HBCU presidents, but I think most public school presidents will say funding is one of the major things that we all see. Without funding you can't go into some of the programs you know that there is a market for sometimes, and it just limits you. (Dr. Lyelle Boutte, personal communication, September 26, 2005)

I guess just because of the climate in higher education right now you have the intense competition for students. Predominantly White institutions have better fiscal resources so they're able to actually buy students. The example I use is Texas A&M because there's a big article on them in the *Chronicle [of Higher Education]*. I want to say in the fall, where the president said look, Texas A& M does not look like the state of Texas in terms of diversity so we're about to fix this up. And of the things they have is a half a million dollars that they can use so that if they offer a scholarship to a student and the student is going somewhere else, they can dump more money on that student. It's just a bidding war. So that's happening with students, and it's also happening with faculty and staff. I know a lot of your HBCU campuses you're seeing aging faculty because the younger, newer scholars are going after . . . you know they want to get paid. The average salaries at the Black schools are much smaller so they are going to go where the money is, and if the big White schools have the money and they really want the Black scholar, that's who they are going to get. Those become the mission, the major obstacles in terms of the intense competition for faculty, staff, and students, and a lot of that is predicated on how much money you have. Unfortunately HBCUs don't have the financial resources to compete in that game. (Dr. Earl Davis, personal communication, August 2, 2005)

Overall, financial constraints contribute to the ongoing struggles that presidents of HBCUs experience. The lack of adequate funds prohibits them from creating innovative academic programs that will attract more students. Due to insufficient funds, schools have to raise the cost of tuition, which makes the idea of pursuing higher education an unattainable goal for some students. Financial constraints hinder Black colleges from competing with predominantly White institutions because they cannot contend, for example, with those institutions' sprawling facilities and faculty salaries. Black colleges and universities were developed as separate and unequal institutions compared to predominantly White schools. The perpetual challenge of not having sufficient funding continues to cripple HBCUs and places them at a considerable disadvantage.

One of the 15 presidents participating in the study, however, stated that financial constraints do not interfere with mission implementation. Dr. Scales Donahoo offered the following response:

> I don't know of any barriers that are insurmountable. I think throughout higher education and throughout the states, and this is not unique to HBCUs, many states are experiencing reducing funding to higher education. State appropriations have been reduced over the last several years. In my experience, that has not been a barrier to us accomplishing our mission. (personal communication, July 7, 2005)

His response says that Black colleges experience the same type of financial cuts as other types of higher education institutions. Based on Dr. Donahoo's experience, the financial constraints are not an unmanageable challenge. This perspective attests to the resiliency of Black colleges and the presidents who lead them. In spite of the difficulty, they persevere.

### Resistance to Change

While the presidents revealed that financial constraints are the primary source of struggle for Black colleges, they also said that people employed at these institutions are resistant to change. Change is often an uncomfortable experience for people because they fear the unknown. As presidents attempt to stay current and competitive in the higher education system, they have to be open to new possibilities and ways of doing things. Unfortunately, they have to convince their support staff that change will benefit, not hurt the institutions. A few of the presidents in the study shared the following:

> Sometimes the unwillingness to change is a challenge. Sometimes the status quo, the existing programs, the existing activities that you have that have been long term at the university, those programs and activities tend to consume resources. And once you lock resources in, it is kind of difficult to move them around to address new and emerging needs and issues and concerns. (Dr. Bobby Isaac, personal communication, July 12, 2005)

> There are always going to be people who view . . . you will see where there are folk who are saying, we don't need to be recruiting Hispanic students. I don't want to take up all your time but I would argue the very comments that they are making were the comments that some Whites made about folk like me going to the University of Kentucky back in 1968. I keep saying that you all ought to be ashamed of yourselves to say those things because it's not true. These folk will enhance our institutions; they won't take anything away from our institutions. That is one challenge, that there are many people who don't see the need for that. (Dr. Kerry Foster, personal communication, August 12, 2005)

> I think that one of things that our campuses as HBCUs are particularly crippled with is a very high level of resistance to change. You may be familiar with the crabs-in-the-barrel phenomenon. There's a lot of internal resistance to forward movement on our campuses. (Dr. Sultan Rovaris, personal communication, August 15, 2005)

> The one challenge is the continuing disbelief of significant players in the process. A people's depth of degradation often puts blinders on them about their potential future and causes them to want to take slower, more careful, fearful steps or, in some cases, no steps at all, but to hold on to what they believe has been the accomplishment of the past. So disbelief among significant players is one major barrier. A second major challenge is really the intent to destroy by members in power and the majority community, and in some cases those in the minority community who have issues with direction and vision, or with personalities, or with what they have experienced in the past, or what they perceive to be their own power mispositioning. The third major barrier is, inasmuch as we primarily serve in a press community, there is really only one generation that has enjoyed legal equality.

The resources that the alumni of that community can bring to bear are always less than one one-thousandth of what can be brought to bear by the alumni of other kinds of institutions. The ability to compete on several fronts is circumscribed by the outcomes of history. (Dr. Jared Auguste, personal communication, July 20, 2005)

The general sentiment of the presidents is that individuals find comfort in what has worked for Black colleges in the past, remain proud of their legacy and accomplishments, and prefer to avoid change and the chance to improve. This resistance to change occurs because many Black college employees have occupied their positions for a considerable time and they do not recognize the new needs of the institution. As a result, HBCUs do not experience growth, which precludes them from being able to compete with other colleges and universities across the nation. Presidents, therefore, have to create a comfortable balance between preserving the history of Black colleges and universities and, simultaneously, moving them in new directions.

## Is the Mission Unique?

Historically Black colleges and universities are not restricted to African American students. Ultimately, students decide whether they want to attend a Black school or choose from a host of other options. Historically Black colleges and universities are a piece of the larger puzzle of the American higher education system. The challenge, however, is that these particular schools disproportionately carry the burden of having to justify their existence (Brown & Freeman, 2002; Brown et al., 2004; Fleming, 1984; Garibaldi, 1984). Consequently, Black colleges continue to fight to convince the world of their unique role. The interview question posed to the presidents in the study was, "Based on your experience, do you believe that historically Black institutions have a unique mission in comparison to other types of higher education institutions?" This section details the common themes that emerged in the presidents' responses to the unique character of HBCUs. While many of the responses overlap, the two themes include overcoming obstacles and preserving culture.

### Overcoming Obstacles

Black colleges and universities operate in the face of considerable obstacles. The presidents in the study offer their perspectives on how these obstacles give Black schools a unique identity and role in the larger academy.

There's no question in my mind that they do [have a unique mission]. I mentioned the fact that we admit students who would not be admissible in some other institutions. Generally speaking, tuition and costs are lower [here], and we provide an environment where we are willing to take students from where they are, to take them to where they need to be, which is not always the case on predominantly White campuses. Generally speaking, we provide a sense of leadership development opportunities that are not available for students of African decent on predominantly White campuses. For example, at [Giovanni State University] we have over 80 student organizations, and any Black student on the campus has an opportunity to serve in a leadership role in those organizations; whereas, on the predominantly White campus, it would be much more competitive and difficult for Black students to get involved in those organizations. The other thing is that some of our campuses provide a sense of reservoir of Black culture, if you will, that you typically would not find on predominantly White campuses. So there are some uniquenesses that I think continue to distinguish HBCUs and continue to argue for their perseverance. (Dr. Sultan Rovaris, personal communication, August 15, 2005)

Yes is the major answer; but any institution that accepts poor people, people without personal resources where family income is not abundant to contribute to the education, any institution that accepts students who went to high school and elementary school that are not of the best quality, any institution that is handicapped by the lack of facilities and operating budgets will have areas that are weak or needing. I must hasten to say that Black institutions have produced the major numbers of Black professionals in this country. Even if these students go on to majority institutions for their graduate and professional work, many of the Black leaders we are looking at today had their beginnings in a humble Black college someplace. One of the things I never do, and I would encourage you not to do that, is to judge HBCUs from their deficiencies, which is lack of money. What we lack in money we certainly compensate for in spirit, in cultural preservation, in the ability to retain and motivate, in the historical proof that we are a vital force in educating the world. We had African students at Black colleges long before Africa became popular. . . . The fact is that there are so many strengths at these institutions where we achieve our goals despite the shortage of funds that I would encourage people to spin it around and begin to look at our historic contributions to this country and our ability to sustain ourselves despite all kinds of things that could make us angry. But like Desmond Tutu says, "There is no future without forgiveness."

After we recognize the challenges we face, we just sit up later, work harder, and encourage other people to do the same. (Dr. Mathilda Marie, personal communication, July 29,2005)

Well, the uniqueness, if you want to call it that, lies in who you provide access to. Your uniqueness in my view boils down to access, and that is you are trying to provide access to young people who may not otherwise be able to get into college and universities that have more restricted access that's based on the criteria that we use these days in selecting our student bodies. So, yes, two things are unique about historically Black colleges. One is the access that you provide to young people, and, believe me, access is not universal across all historically Black colleges either. . . . The second part of our uniqueness is the success rate at which we graduate young people from our universities and put them into the workforce as competitive candidates. (Devon Lamard, personal communication, August 16, 2005)

In a sense, maybe not as unique, but I think they have a special mission because HBCUs are still drawing from the marketplace of first-generation college entrance, which is different from some institutions. Many of our students who come to us don't have the advantage of being exposed to country clubs or being exposed to a variety of career choices. Many of them didn't even believe until someone told them that college was a viable option to them. They don't have the advantage of being surrounded by magazines that deal with world affairs. They don't have the advantage of having the kind of people in their homes to talk about that you can be a judge or you can be a lawyer. That's beginning to change, but a lot of our institutions . . . we still draw from a marketplace of young people who are the first people in their families to ever seek a college education. For small communities, we're their hope; we are that link with the opportunity. I often say here [Winfrey College] has really educated and graduated some of the foremost leaders in this country and even abroad. We have alumni who live in Switzerland and South Africa, West Africa and other European countries, but still, those people came from small communities. I often say to them that our institutions, the historically Black colleges and universities, must be able to swing on the doors of hope and opportunity, and we must be able to afford these young people at least a chance to have a seat at the broad table of human opportunity. And that's what I look at us, the role is saying, sometimes we take these young people from nowhere USA and we take them somewhere globally. We help them to stretch their reach and expand their minds to all the possibilities that are out here and help them to believe and realize the American dream. (Mary Frances, personal communication, August 15, 2005)

The presidents attest to the reality that Black colleges function with disadvantages. Students enter campuses and are often not prepared academically. They are from poor family backgrounds and have not been exposed to life outside their present circumstance. Some of the students are first-generation college students and are unaware of the full possibilities of their educational training. In addition to the disadvantages students bring to Black college campuses, the institutions possess their own set of challenges. In spite of all this, HBCUs persevere. They are unique because they provide students with leadership development opportunities they would not be able to experience on predominantly White campuses. According to the presidents, Black colleges are responsible for educating many of the African American leaders of this country. Historically Black colleges continue to contribute to the world by producing African American professionals, in general, who have a positive impact on the world.

## Preservation of Culture

Black colleges and universities possess a distinct academic culture (Brown 2002b; Freeman, 1998). The following presidents' responses address the notion that Black colleges have a unique identity and overall environment that contributes to the positive experience of their students.

Absolutely. We are at the heart of the educational enterprise. We're also the institution in whatever communities we reside that has the most profound understanding of the local condition and culture of the minority community and therefore is best positioned to impact that. We're also the primary preservers and purveyors of the culture and history of the African American community, and done right, we are the best possible laboratories for the final address to the questions of what constitutes an appropriate address to American diversity. (Dr. Jared Auguste, personal communication, July 20, 2005)

I do. I do think that the fact that we are the only historically African American institution in the state . . . and there are about 30 plus others. We, the public presidents, all come together every month. The presidents will tell me often that they cannot do for their Black students what we can do. It's the environment. You see, they can get them a degree; they can get a degree as they can get a degree here. But [Walker University] gives them that empowerment that you can hardly define; it's the sense of belonging and ownership. They cannot even when they try, and they do. I'm not talking about acceptance, I'm not talking about segregation, I'm talking about nothing but the environment. All [Walker University] is doing is the same things the other schools are doing, but it's the environment that makes the difference. At [Walker University] it is a choice for all students here in the state . . . and for Black students particularly. We find that many Black students who come to [Walker University] and get their undergraduate degree really move into the major universities with so much more self-confidence, and they move on successfully. I think it's that empowerment: I can achieve. (Dr. Trevis Freeman, personal communication, July 7, 2005)

Now, let me be perfectly honest with you. I think the question that people raise about whether or not Black colleges have a unique mission is an uninformed question because the same raisers of those questions don't raise the question on whether or not Catholic colleges have a unique mission or whether Jewish colleges have a unique mission, but they tend to ask it about Black colleges. Now, having said that, there is a significantly unique mission, and part of that is to keep actively alive the sense of history, tradition, and culture of African American contributions to this nation and the world. In addition to providing quality academic education, its mission is also as a repository of history, culture, and tradition. (Dr. Nathan Dudley, personal communication, July 20, 2005)

Historically Black colleges and universities possess a unique understanding of the condition of African American people. Black schools acknowledge and celebrate the culture and history of Black students. This type of environment empowers them and gives them a greater sense of confidence. This nurturing environment helps students to believe that they are capable of succeeding. Dr. Nathan Dudley asserts that Black colleges should not be questioned about their role in the higher education because they have already proven they are significant institutions.

## *Providing Role Models*

One president in the study shared a unique perspective on identifying the unique mission of HBCUs. Although some of his response coincided with the other presidents' perspectives, he suggested that Black colleges are unique because they provide students with role models.

> There is a niche, a place for historically Black schools, just like there are for religious schools, just like there are for major research, just like there are for small colleges. Here is what I believe: I believe that there is really something to the role model effect of seeing people of color in positions from A to Z. I think if you go pick your school, they ought to talk about their legacy, their history and so forth. Well, it's important for students to hear that about ours as well. Again, while I'm sure that every school will say they provide leadership opportunities for students, and I'm not doubting that, but I'm not so sure if the Black students I encounter here from top to bottom in leadership positions would be in those same positions at some of the predominantly White schools. I didn't say that there wouldn't be any in there; of course, there would be. I really do believe that we give them some opportunities to be involved, engaged, and so forth in a way that they might not get. Just by the same token I bet you Smith and Mount Holyoke and so forth does some of the same things for women. These women could be leaders at Princeton or anywhere, but I think Mount Holyoke and Smith might give them more opportunity and I think that is what [Shabazz University] might do for Black folk. (Dr. Kerry Foster, personal communication, August 12, 2005)

The presence of African American role models enables students to see the manifestation of hard work and dedication in the lives of the African American leaders on their campuses. They are able to see themselves in their professors and the administration; this is a unique contribution of Black colleges. Both predominantly White institutions and HBCUs employ African Americans. The difference, however, is that students on Black college campuses are able to witness African Americans in high positions such as department chair, dean, vice president for academic affairs, and, ultimately, president.

## The Relevance of the Historic Mission

The historic mission of Black colleges refers to the idea that the initial purpose of these institutions was to educate African American students when most existing colleges and universities were not open to them. Recognizing that African Americans no longer suffer from legal restrictions, and that Black colleges themselves experience mandates for increased racial diversity, this study asked the presidents if the historic mission remains relevant. They shared the following:

> I think that the key word is access. I am not sure that we want to limit it only to African Americans because there are a number of citizens in our nation whose backgrounds and socioeconomic standings are quite similar to that of African Americans. So I think our institutions are committed and dedicated to providing access to educational opportunities irrespective of the ethnic background of the individual. (Dr. Bobby Isaac, personal communication, July 12, 2005)

> It is still primarily on African American students, but the thing is, historically Black colleges have never excluded Whites or anybody else. One of the reasons that they have remained predominantly African American has been a factor of the choices that non-African Americans have made not to attend. (Dr. Nathan Dudley, personal communication, July 20, 2005)

> I think for the most part there are some exceptions. There are a number of schools like West Virginia College, Kentucky State that are approximately 50% White. Frankly, I don't know the extent to which they continue with any part of their admission related to students of African descent. I suspect that there is some continuance of that, but for the most part I think that HBCUs continue to be HBCUs and continue to focus on their primary clientele, students of African decent. (Dr. Sultan Rovaris, personal communication August 15, 2005)

> Yes. As long as the conditions in society persist, the need for Black colleges will always be there. Nobody questions the legitimacy of a religious college, a military college, or any other specialized college and so [on] until this society is such that the need no longer exists, I would say yes, it is. . . . My institution is loaded with White kids whose family income is no greater than that of the Blacks. The poor White people that some people would call other names, and I don't name call, but you know the term for White people such as hillbillies, trailer park, White trash, all of that. The profile of these students is the same [as] for poor Black students, and don't forget now that in Black education you have Hampton and Spelman and Howard and [University of Angelou] that have some kids here who can posture and drive their Mercedes to class and go sailing when they go home and fly to

Europe, the French Riviera for their vacation. Don't forget now that Black is not a word that means downtrodden, daddy left home, mother had 10 children, it doesn't mean that. The Black middle class is what Zora Neale Hurston called, "the best kept secret," in an essay she wrote in 1938 and it is true. Go to Bennett College and look what's inside of their cafeteria; they have woodwork to make your mouth water. Go to any of these institutions [and] you'll find artwork and historical pieces. You see, we have to struggle with this business of image. . . . If some people ever saw how Black people live for real in their homes, they would deny us opportunity because they would think we're moving too fast or moving out of the place that sociology has created for us. So I hasten to say, Black does not mean poor, downtrodden, and it means Condoleezza Rice, it means Colin Powell. The world sees the sniper kid or the drug addict or someone who holds you up; that's what the world sees, and that's their choice to codify us. (Dr. Mathilda Marie, personal communication, July 29, 2005)

Yeah, I think it is, but part of what's happening is that because we're losing so many to the majority institutions, more and more people are talking about, well, we need to get into the Hispanic market. So, when I hear that here, I don't jump up and down, I'm saying, "I don't think we've competed for Black students." That's my thing. We stopped competing and I'm not willing just to say, well, because people are just trying to figure out how do we pay the bills, let's try to get Hispanic students. But then you get a critical mass of Hispanic students, it'll be Bluefield [State University] but it'll be just a different population, you'll have more Hispanics. It will be an HBCU that's mostly Hispanic, and that will happen. I think that we have to start competing for the students, and we've got to be able to succinctly say this is what we do better than other folks, and this is how we show we do it. (Dr. Earl Davis, personal communication, August 2, 2005)

Yes, our focus is still on African American students. One of the things I say here is that we want to make sure that we encourage diversity on our campus, geographically, racial, gender wise, and all of that. But we have to also respect the historic mission of the college. We don't change it because the world might be changing because there still is a real place for an institution like ours. And I think that more historically Black colleges and universities must respect and maintain ownership of that historic mission. So often we want to become the images of our sister institutions that are predominantly White and those that are Ivy League and those that are better endowed. It does not mean that you don't really ascribe to growth in your institutions, but to realize that within that same content and context you can offer a quality education and a quality environment to steal a specific population of students. I am committed to making sure that these young people will have access to higher education. I feel very strongly that if we fail at our institutions to provide the opportunity for these young people to receive a higher education, then we've failed; we fail our society and we fail America in a sense . . . if we don't educate these young people, 50 years from today, our democracy will perhaps look like those countries that we are sending our sons and daughters in to defend and protect. We are educating, all of our institutions of higher education, but more particular our historically Black colleges and universities, are the preservers and keepers of the American promise and also of sustaining a vibrant democracy where all citizens have an opportunity to participate equally. (Mary Frances, personal communication, August 15, 2005)

I would say that back then many of them [Black colleges] were designed to provide services to Whites. If you look at the fact that they were creating mechanics, homemakers, and cooks with emphasis on the industrial arts . . . while that could benefit Blacks, it also was a benefit to Whites and it was also to create citizens for White America. The interesting thing I would argue about an HBCU back during the . . . 1880s and so on, was that Whites supported them and Blacks did, but they may have been supporting them for different reasons. Whites could see them as being beneficial and maybe creating docile people and so forth. Blacks could see this as leading to freedom in a certain way. Even though the curriculum may have been dominated with White thinking at some period of time in some schools, Black people were nevertheless able to turn that around; it was better than no school . . . (Dr. Kerry Foster, personal communication, August 12, 2005)

The majority of the presidents identified the historic mission of HBCUs as a relevant mission today. Although a few schools that are categorized as HBCUs maintain a predominantly White student enrollment, overall, Black colleges remain committed to serving African American students. The presidents point out, however, that Black colleges are not discriminatory institutions and that they welcome all students, irrespective of race. The problem, as stated by Dr. Nathan Dudley, is that non-African Americans choose not to attend HBCUs. Black colleges, therefore, have to compete for the best and brightest students, and Dr. Earl Davis argues that rather than looking to the Hispanic student population, Black colleges need to focus on recruiting African American students. The historic mission of educating African Americans continues to be a priority among presidents of HBCUs.

# 5

# THE MORE THINGS CHANGE, THE MORE THEY STAY THE SAME

This final chapter provides recommendations for policy and practice. The results of this research study provide some insights into the ways Black college presidents define and implement the missions of their institutions. Additionally, the study identifies critical challenges that presidents of historically Black college and universities (HBCUs) face as they attempt to preserve the legacy and maintain the relevance of these institutions in the larger higher education system. Just as this study answers some questions about the topic of mission, it also raises important questions and concerns. What did the presidents in the study *not* say? What themes were not identified?

The research findings indicate matters that presidents of these institutions should focus on as they lead these colleges and universities in a higher education environment that continues to devalue their contributions. Likewise, this research also highlights some issues related to HBCUs that remain under-researched and need more attention from both policy analysts and educational scholars. The future of Black colleges depends on ongoing assessment of their current condition to make meaningful improvement.

## The Difficulty in Defining Mission

The term *mission* refers to an institution's explicit role, purpose, and function within the larger system of higher education. The overarching question posed to the presidents in the study was, "How do you personally define the mission of your college or university?" Assumed to be simple and direct, this question turned out to be somewhat difficult for the presidents to answer. Although the participants received a copy of all of the questions before the interview, this particular one elicited a slight pause or hesitation before the presidents responded. Following this awkward silence, the presidents began to discuss, and often recite, their official school mission statements.

Approximately 7 of the 15 presidents found it difficult to articulate a personal definition of mission because they could not disconnect from their institutions' mission statements. Mission statements have power because they are symbolic and represent an ingrained fabric of a college or university's identity. This study, however, forced the presidents to engage in what Weick (1995) identifies as sensemaking. As detailed in the conceptual framework, sensemaking simply means to make sense of something.

Sensemaking is concerned with the ways in which individuals construct meaning and generate interpretations. Sensemaking is a useful lens for the purpose of this study because it makes the presidents process and organize their thoughts about mission, independent of the actual mission statements. The responses, therefore, represent an introspective analysis of mission and reflect what Brown (2003) identifies as an *emic* approach to researching HBCUs. The data from an emic approach are valuable because they provide information on Black colleges from an insider's perspective.

In addition to the difficulty in defining mission, the presidents in the study experienced difficulty in discussing the mission of their respective schools without including other HBCUs. They often spoke in terms of "we" and "our institutions" as if to suggest the importance of similarities that unite Black colleges. Dr. Earl Davis, president of Scott King College, likened Black colleges to church hymnals—although some people are Baptist, Episcopalian, or Methodist, they all sing from the same hymnbooks.

Although a simple word, *mission* has a complex meaning. The meaning is complex because the term embodies myriad considerations, particularly in regard to higher education institutions. According to Hendrickson (1991), colleges and universities establish relationships with numerous constituencies, including government and the public at large. These relationships bind institutions to a commitment to provide academic learning and instruction for students. In turn, these commitments influence how the presidents conceptualize and implement mission. In their attempts to define mission, presidents have to ask the tough questions: Why do we exist? What purpose do we serve? How do our HBCUs contribute to the larger system of higher education? As evidenced in the results of the research, the answers to these tough questions represent what the presidents in the study value about their institutions. The responses reveal the presidents' priorities; however, the results do not reflect the totality of the mission of Black colleges. The presidents in the study are a sample of presidents who lead four-year, Black colleges. Their perspectives on mission, therefore, are not generalizable to all HBCUs or other higher education institutions.

## Unique Colleges with Common Missions

The majority of research on HBCUs directly states or indirectly implies that Black colleges serve a unique mission in comparison to other types of higher education institutions. The review of the literature indicates that Black colleges and universities provide African American students with an empowering educational experience with which predominantly White institutions remain unable to compete. At the time when HBCUs were founded, their mission of specifically serving African American students did make them unique because few other colleges and universities made any effort to admit or educate these individuals. On the surface, the results of this research further support the belief that Black colleges serve a unique mission based on the responses of the presidents.

Most of the presidents eagerly proclaimed that Black colleges do serve a unique mission and effortlessly explained the reasons why. A few of the presidents said that Black colleges are not different from other higher education institutions, but they also proceeded to detail the special qualities that HBCUs possess. In the modern higher education landscape, federal, state, and institution antidiscrimination policies make what was once a unique college mission now appear to be an antiquated purpose. Further analysis of the presidents' responses reveals that Black colleges and universities do not serve a unique mission, but their mission *matters* because they cater to a special population of student learners who continue to need services and assistance that other types of institutions fail to make available to them.

Although two of the universities represented in the study (Jemison State University and Waters University) maintain a predominantly White student population, most Black colleges primarily educate and serve African American students. The focus on this special population of students influences the overall mission of the college or university as the leaders of these institutions seek to provide the best services based on the needs of their student bodies. As Freeman (1998) suggests, Black colleges maintain a distinct campus culture. Black colleges and universities are aware of and understand the critical needs of Black students. When the presidents in the study defined the mission of their respective schools, they discussed matters applicable to all higher education institutions. In general, colleges and universities: (a) provide access and opportunities for learning, (b) prepare students for leadership roles, and (c) equip students to transition successfully into graduate and professional schools. If the focus shifts away from African American students, the mission of HBCUs mirrors that of other types of colleges and universities.

A few of the presidents found the question concerning the unique role of Black colleges to be somewhat offensive. Their attitude stemmed from the harsh reality that HBCUs disproportionately carry the burden of having to justify their existence. The presidents reaffirmed Benjamin E. Mays's (1978) argument that other types of institutions, such as Catholic colleges, for example, do not receive the type of scrutiny that Black colleges endure. The presidents' attitudes echoed Charles V. Willie's (1994) assertion that HBCUs have yet to convince the general public of their role and overall significance, despite their proven success. The reasoning behind this scrutiny is that HBCUs did not start on an equal playing field within mainstream higher education. Black colleges were created as separate and unequal higher education institutions, and predominantly White institutions continue to dominate and control the playing field, especially in graduate and professional education. The challenge for presidents and other supporters of Black colleges is recognizing that these racially identifiable institutions will continue to face questions concerning mission. As this study indicates, the solution is providing information about the purpose, role, and function of Black colleges from credible sources, such as the presidents of these colleges and universities.

Despite the presidents' resentment about having their institutions identified as unique, or the implication that these schools are not as good as their predominantly White counterparts, the study participants proudly acknowledged the special qualities endemic to their respective schools. Historically Black colleges face many obstacles, yet they continue to persevere. For example, many of these institutions lack adequate financial resources, which can prevent them from maintaining updated learning facilities or using current technology. In spite of such resource limitations, these institutions succeed in preparing and positioning African American students for future achievement.

In essence, the struggle of Black colleges is their trademark. Yet, similar to the struggle of African American people in the United States, the struggle of HBCUs reflects their strength and resiliency as they continue to do more with less. Black colleges provide Black students with an academic environment that respects and celebrates their culture and history. The celebration on these campuses is not limited to the month of February, but, rather, is acknowledged throughout the year and incorporated into the curriculum and daily activities. Another special quality of Black colleges is their ability to provide positive African American role models for students. Students have opportunities to observe African Americans occupying all facets of the faculty and administration. Perhaps the greatest quality of HBCUs is their ability to enroll academically underprepared students and transform them into college graduates. As Kannerstein (1978) contends, Black colleges are more concerned with what happens to students after they leave the campuses than with what the students bring to the campus in their freshman year. In doing so, Black colleges and universities remain committed to a service mission that focuses on serving the whole needs of students as people by preparing to succeed in both college and in life. The mission of HBCUs matters to the African American community because these institutions represent a constant reminder that higher education is an attainable goal.

## The Servant Leader

The service element of the Black college mission is very important to the individuals who lead these schools. Dr. Clarence Myers, president of Morrison State University, suggested that being the president of an HBCU is similar to being the pastor of a large church. This analogy coincided with the research results on the presidents' perceptions of their role in implementing the mission of their college or university. Similar to the relationship a pastor has with a church congregation, presidents of Black colleges view themselves as the visible representatives of their schools. Both pastors and presidents represent the face and voice of their respective institutions. Pastors and presidents also engage in strategic planning to accomplish specific goals.

The key is that neither of these types of leaders can reach their goals in isolation, but must surround themselves with a cooperative and competent team to be successful.

Essentially, presidents of Black colleges and universities use what Robert Greenleaf (1977) identifies as servant leadership. The basic principle of servant leadership is that a great leader is a servant first and a leader second. Despite the challenges and negative perceptions that plague these institutions, many of the presidents in the study stated that they deliberately chose to lead an HBCU. These individuals simply recognized the need and desired to serve. Presidents of Black colleges remain committed to serving their institutions by considering their students' needs as their first priority. As servant leaders, Black college presidents implement the missions of their institutions through collaborative efforts as they welcome input from faculty, students, alumni, and the general public.

In addition to presidents of Black colleges being servant leaders, these individuals promote the notion of servant leadership on their campuses. Throughout the interviews, presidents stressed the importance of providing students with a sense of responsibility to give of themselves. While Black colleges give students the academic tools for individual success, they also encourage them to be active in community service to uplift the condition of all African American people. In doing so, these servant leaders not only ensure that their institutions effectively prepare students to achieve professional and personal success, but also to fulfill the public service mission attached to higher education in general by instilling their students with skills and the desire to use their education to uplift and benefit others. Historically Black colleges must strive to be to students what the Black church is to Black people—a place of forgiveness and hope.

## Race: The Salient Yet Silent Theme

Historically Black colleges and universities are undeniably racially identifiable higher education institutions. Although all Black colleges do not have a dominant African American student enrollment, the inescapable assumption is that these schools are populated with persons of African descent. A school that is identified as liberal arts, doctoral-granting, or community, for example, immediately conjures up ideas about their focus and the type of education they provide. The federal designation of a school as an HBCU, on the other hand, shifts the attention from *what* is being offered to *whom* it is being offered to. Any discussion of Black colleges is incomplete without addressing the issue of race. A few of the presidents in the study mention race, but they do not explore or expose the topic fully in a meaningful manner. Race emerged as the salient, yet silent theme.

The topic of race and understanding the implications of race is critically important, particularly as it relates to the mission of HBCUs. This research study defines mission as the overall role, purpose, and function of higher education institutions. The first step in understanding mission (or the current state of any phenomenon) requires an examination of the history of these institutions. How did these particular colleges and universities come to be? The history literature paints a very vivid picture of Black colleges and universities being borne of necessity as a means to educate former enslaved men, women, and their progeny. Black colleges developed during a tumultuous time of racial tension and segregation as laws precluded African American people from acquiring an education. The root of the problem was and continues to be the matter of race and the pervasiveness of racism that dictates the way of the world.

The presidents in the study effortlessly communicated the class argument about the obstacles of Black colleges and how these institutions are at a considerable disadvantage when compared to their predominantly White counterparts. When asked to identify the challenges that hinder mission implementation, the presidents overwhelmingly agreed that Black colleges lack adequate financial resources. Historically Black colleges and universities are often unable to compete with many higher education institutions because they are not in a financial position to recruit top-quality faculty, improve building facilities, and broaden course offerings. Surely the class issue is a valid one, but what about race? Race is like the big elephant in the room that all of the presidents see, but act as if it is invisible. Race is the invisible elephant that explains why Black colleges are often perceived negatively. Race is the unidentified theme that clarifies why these schools are heavily scrutinized and criticized. Race is the unnamed fact that exposes the huge discrepancy in how funds are distributed among Black versus predominantly White colleges and universities. Race is the unspoken truth that reveals why studies on the college presidency only include presidents of Black colleges in the periphery. Race is the hidden reason why Black colleges are often not found in the *US News and World Report* rankings. Ultimately, race is the salient, yet silent theme.

A few of the presidents in the study mentioned the race factor, but they quickly moved on to the next part of the dialogue. In discussing the many challenges associated with leading HBCUs, noticeably missing from the transcripts was any direct reference to racism, racial discrimination, or racial prejudice. Why was this the case? Perhaps the matter of race remained relatively absent because the presidents did not find it pertinent to the topic at hand. Perhaps the presidents in the study held back because they did not know the researcher or the intentions of the research and feared their words could be matched with identity. The problem is, their silence suggests that race is not an important issue. The politically correct thing to do is to pretend that the world is color-blind and that Black people have overcome issues of past social oppressions. The reality is that race is powerful; it dictates, divides, and conquers. Historically Black colleges and universities, as a result, continue to deal with the repercussions of race's wrath.

## Concluding Thoughts

The mission of HBCUs is intricately woven into the history of the institutions. The rich history of Black colleges continues to influence the ways in which presidents define and implement mission. Individuals interested in attaining the college presidency at Black colleges must be aware of the cultural traditions, legacy, language, and overall focus that these institutions value because these things infiltrate all aspects of campus life. The presidency at Black colleges requires an inherent desire to serve and a deliberate commitment to overcoming obstacles.

Historically Black colleges and universities erroneously attempt to emulate traditional higher education institutions, particularly in the way these schools relate to their student populations. Federal and state diversity initiatives are rampant and Black colleges are the primary targets of desegregation initiatives. African American researchers such as Charles V. Willie (1994) and Sebrenia Sims (1994) advocate the need for Black colleges to become more racially diverse. More specifically, both agree that HBCUs should deliberately recruit White students. Willie (1994) audaciously states that Black colleges are not only for Black people, and that these institutions should maintain a 20% White student population. What about Hispanic and Asian students? Why are these students not the focus of diversity initiatives? Undoubtedly the push toward diversity is a noble act, but the challenging question is, "How much is enough?" First the argument is for a minimum 20% White student presence, but the expectation will slowly but surely increase. What will the future of HBCUs look like? They will ultimately lose their identity as cultural repositories for African American people. Black colleges will stray from the historic mission for which they were founded. Rather than trying to mimic traditional colleges and universities, HBCUs must take pride in their special niche in the larger higher education system and continue to preserve the legacy of providing access and opportunity specifically to African American students.

Historically Black colleges must continue to focus on African American students, as they are often underserved at majority colleges and universities. For many African American students, Black colleges are their only option, and leaders of these institutions must not lose sight of this special-needs population. Black colleges must accept this responsibility and continue to make provisions for students who lack proper academic preparation but possess great potential. If HBCUs do not cater to this population, who will? In addition to serving students with poor academic preparation, Black colleges must become more active in recruiting high-achieving African American students. Historically Black colleges and universities have to be more assertive in making sure that these students are aware of the opportunities and services available.

For Black colleges to continue to prosper, presidents, administrators, and faculty have to find ways to encourage students to return to and support their alma maters. Sixty percent of the presidents in the study received an undergraduate degree from an HBCU. This finding suggests that their experiences as students at Black colleges played a role in their decision to become leaders of these institutions. The future of Black colleges depends on graduates of Black colleges. Who knows these institutions better than the individuals who learn, live, and work at these colleges and universities? Who better to lead Black colleges than individuals who genuinely care about and have a vested interest in their prosperity? Concurring with the testimony of Dr. Mathilda Marie, president of University of Angelou, individuals bloom where they are planted.

The public at large may never be convinced of the mission or usefulness of Black colleges. Presidents and other supporters of these institutions must not take offense, but rather embrace this experience as an opportunity to educate others about the contributions of these colleges and universities. Another way to inform the public at large of the contributions of these institutions is through comprehensive academic research. Scholars need to investigate Black colleges in a more systematic manner to attain accurate and reliable information that not only demonstrates what these institutions do, but also offers some direction in helping them to better fulfill their mission. Further research should explore the official mission statements of Black colleges. Because presidents in this study found it difficult to disconnect from their mission statements, research is needed to examine whether there is congruence between how presidents of Black colleges define mission and what the mission statements dictate. Also, many of the presidents in the study mentioned the important role that mentors played in their career development. Future studies should also examine this relationship and uncover how these mentors affected their careers.

This book reignites the topic of mission started by W.E.B. Du Bois and Booker T. Washington. Borrowing the words of Dr. Bobby Isaac, president of Bassett State University, HBCUs are an oasis in the jungle; ultimately their mission matters. The results of this research study provide a glimpse into this multidimensional topic from the presidents of these four-year institutions. The ways in which the leaders define, and face the challenges associated with mission and overcome them suggest that Black colleges are a critical piece of the larger American higher education puzzle. The assertion that HBCUs offer a common mission does not negate the unique qualities they possess, nor does it seek to belittle their contributions. Historically Black colleges serve a necessary function as they educate and graduate a significant number of African American students.

# REFERENCES

Allen, W. R. (1992). The color of success: African American college student outcomes at predominantly white and historically black public colleges and universities. *Harvard Educational Review, 62*(1), 26–44.

Allen, W. R., Epps, E. G., & Haniff, N. Z. (Eds.). (1991). *College in black and white: African American students in predominantly white and in historically black public universities.* Albany, NY: State University of New York Press.

Allen, W. R., & Jewell, J. O. (2002). A backward glance forward: Past, present, and future perspectives on historically black colleges and universities. *The Review of Higher Education, 25*(3), 241–261.

Altbach, P. G. (1991). The racial dilemma in American higher education. In P. G. Altbach & K. Lomotey (Eds.), *The racial crisis in American higher education* (pp. 3–17). New York: State of New York Press.

Bensimon, E. M., Neumann, A., & Birnbaum, R. (1989). *Making sense of administrative leadership: The "L" word in higher education.* ASHE-ERIC Higher Education Reports No 1. Washington, DC: The George Washington University, School of Education and Human Development.

Billingsley, A. (1982). Building strong faculties in black colleges. *Journal of Negro Education, 51*, 4–15.

Birnbaum, R. (1988a). *How colleges work: The cybernetics of academic organization and leadership.* San Francisco: Jossey-Bass.

Birnbaum, R. (1988b). *The implicit leadership theories of college and university presidents.* Paper presented at the national meeting of the Association for the Study of Higher Education, Baltimore, MD.

Birnbaum, R. (1992). *How academic leadership works: Understanding success and failure in the college presidency.* San Francisco: Jossey-Bass.

Birnbaum, R., & Umbach, P. D. (2001). Scholar, steward, spanner, stranger: The four career paths of college presidents. *The Review of Higher Education, 24*(3), 203–217.

Bogdan, R. C., & Biklen, S. K. (1998). *Qualitative research in education: An introduction to theory and methods* (3rd ed.). Needham Heights, MA: Allyn and Bacon.

Bolman, L. G., & Deal, T. E. (1997). *Reframing organizations: Artistry, choice, and leadership* (2nd ed.). San Francisco: Jossey-Bass.

Brown, M. C. (1995). In defense of the public historically black college and its mission. *The National Honors Report, 16*, 34–40.

Brown, M. C. (1999). *The quest to define collegiate desegregation.* Westport, CT: Bergin and Garvey.

Brown, M. C. (2001). Collegiate desegregation and the public black college: A new policy mandate. *Journal of Higher Education, 72,* 46–62.

Brown, M. C. (2002a). Historically black colleges and universities. In J. F. Forest & K. Kinser (Eds.), *Higher education in the United States: An encyclopedia. Volume I (A-L)* (pp. 314–319) Santa Barbara, CA: ABC-CLIO.

Brown, M. C. (2002b). Good intentions: Collegiate desegregation and transdemographic enrollments. *The Review of Higher Education, 25,* 263–280.

Brown, M. C. (2003). Emics and etics of researching black colleges: Applying facts and avoiding fallacies. *New Directions for Institutional Research, 118,* 27–40.

Brown, M. C., Donahoo, S., & Bertrand, R. D. (2001). The black college and the quest for educational opportunity. *Urban Education, 36*(5), 553–571.

Brown, M. C., & Freeman, K. (Eds.). (2002). Research on historically black colleges. *The Review of Higher Education, 25*(3), 237–368.

Brown, M.C., & Freeman, K. (Eds.). (2004). *Black colleges: New perspectives on policy and practice* (pp. xi–xiv). Westport, CT: Praeger.

Brown, M. C., & Hendrickson, R. M. (1997). Public historically black colleges at the crossroads. *Journal for a Just and Caring Education, 3,* 95–113.

Brown, M. C., Ricard, R. B., & Donahoo, S. (2004). The changing role of historically black colleges and universities: Vistas on dual missions, desegregation, and diversity. In M. C. Brown & K. Freeman (Eds.), *Black colleges: New perspectives on policy and practice* (pp. 3–28). Westport, CT: Praeger.

Browning, J. E., & Williams, J. B. (1978). History and goals of black institutions of higher learning. In C. V. Willie & R. R. Edmonds (Eds.), *Black colleges in America* (pp. 68–93). New York: Teachers College Press.

Buchanan, D. A. (1988). *Presidential roles and qualifications: Views from historically black colleges and universities.* Unpublished doctoral dissertation, Oklahoma State University, Stillwater.

Burton, V. S. (2003). *Structured pathways to the presidency: Becoming a research university president.* Unpublished doctoral dissertation, University of Pennsylvania, Philadelphia.

Clark, B. R. (1972). The organizational saga in higher education. *Administrative Science Quarterly, 17,* 179–194.

Coaxum, J. (2001). The misalignment between the Carnegie classifications and black colleges. *Urban Education, 36* (5) 572–584.

Cohen, A. M. (1998). *The shaping of American higher education.* San Francisco: Jossey-Bass.

Cohen, M. D., & March, J. G. (1986). *Leadership and ambiguity: The American college president* (2nd ed.). Boston: Harvard Business School Press.

Conrad, C., Brier, E. M., & Braxton, J. M. (1997). Factors contributing to the matriculation of white students in public HBCUs. *Journal for a Just and Caring Education, 3*, 37–62.

Conrad, C., & Wyer, J. (1980). *Liberal education in transition* (pp. 4–18). ERIC Research, No. 3. Washington, DC: American Association for Higher Education.

Creswell, J. W. (1998). *Qualitative inquiry and research design: Choosing among five traditions.* Thousand Oaks, CA: Sage.

Cross, T., & Slater, R. (1995). The financial footings of the black colleges. *The Journal of Blacks in Higher Education, 6*, 76–79.

Davis, J. E. (1998). Cultural capital and the role of historically black colleges and universities in educational reproduction. In K. Freeman (Ed.), *African American culture and heritage in higher education research and practice* (pp. 143–153). Westport, CT: Praeger.

Denzin, N. K., & Lincoln, Y. S. (2000). (Eds.). *Handbook of qualitative research* (2nd ed.). Thousand Oaks, CA: Sage.

Dexter, L. W. (1970). *Elite and specialized interviewing.* Evanston, IL: Northwestern University Press.

Diener, T. (1985). Job satisfaction and college faculty in two predominantly black institutions. *Journal of Negro Education, 54*(4), 558–565.

Drewry, H. N., & Doermann, H. (2001). *Stand and prosper: Private black colleges and their students.* Princeton, NJ: Princeton University Press.

Drummond, T. (2000). Black schools go white: In search of a good deal, more and more white students enroll at historically black colleges. *Time, 58.*

Duryea, E. (1981). The university and the state: A historical overview. In P. Altbach & R. Berdahl (Eds.), *Higher education in American society* (pp. 13–33). Buffalo, NY: Prometheus.

Ehrlich, T. (1997). Dewey versus Hutchins: The next round. In R. Orrill (Ed.), *Education and democracy* (pp. 225–262). New York: The College Board.

Fiedler, F. E. (1967). *A theory of leadership effectiveness.* New York: McGraw-Hill.

Fisher, J. L. (1984). *Power of the presidency.* New York: Macmillan Publishing.

Fleming, J. (1984). *Blacks in college: A comparative study of students' success in black and in white institutions.* San Francisco: Jossey-Bass.

Fleming, J. (2004). The significance of historically black college choice influences at black colleges. In. M. C. Brown & K. Freeman (Eds.), *Black colleges: New perspectives on policy and practice* (pp. 29–52). Westport, CT: Praeger.

Foner, E. (1988). *Reconstruction: America's unfinished business, 1863–1877.* New York: Harper & Row.

Foster, L. (2001). The not-so-invisible professors: White faculty at the black college. *Urban Education, 36*(5), 611–629.

Foster, L., & Guyden, J. A. (2004). College in black and white: White faculty at black colleges. In. M. C. Brown & K. Freeman (Eds.), *Black colleges: New perspectives on policy and practice* (pp. 119–133). Westport, CT: Praeger.

Foster, L., Guyden, J. A., & Miller, A. L. (1999) (Eds.). *Affirmed action: Essays on the academic and social lives of white faculty at historically black colleges and universities.* Lanham, MD: Rowman & Littlefield.

Fraenkel, J. R., & Wallen, N. E. (2003). *How to design and evaluate research in education* (5th ed.). Boston: McGraw-Hill.

Freeman, K. (1998). African Americans and college choice: Cultural considerations and policy implications. In K. Freeman (Ed.), *African American culture and heritage in higher education research and practice* (pp. 181–194). Westport, CT: Praeger.

Freeman, K. (1999). HBCUs or PWIs? African American high school students' consideration of higher education institution types. *Review of Higher Education, 23*(1), 91–106.

Fries-Britt, S. (2004). The challenging and needs of high-achieving black college students. In. M. C. Brown & K. Freeman (Eds.), *Black colleges: New perspectives on policy and practice* (pp. 161–175). Westport, CT: Praeger.

Garibaldi, A. (Ed.). (1984). *Black colleges and universities: Challenges for the future.* New York: Praeger.

Geiger, R. (1999). The ten generations of American higher education. In P. Altbach, R. Berdahl, & P. Gumport (Eds.), *American higher education in the twenty-first century: Social, political, and economic challenges* (pp. 38–69). Baltimore: Johns Hopkins University Press.

Geiger, R. (2000). The era of multipurpose colleges in American higher education, 1850–1890. In R. Geiger (Ed.), *The American college in the nineteenth century* (pp. 127–152). Nashville, TN: Vanderbilt University Press.

Greenleaf, R. K. (1977). *Servant leadership: A journey into the nature of legitimate power and greatness.* Ramsey, NJ: Paulist Press.

Hartley, M. (2002). *A call to purpose: Mission-centered change at three liberal arts colleges.* Studies in Higher Education Dissertation Series. New York: RoutledgeFarmer.

Harvey, W. B. (Ed.) (1999). *Grass roots and glass ceilings: African American administrators in predominantly white colleges and universities.* New York: SUNY Press.

Hendrickson, R. M. (1991). The colleges, their constituencies and the courts. *NOLPE Monograph/Book Series*, No. 43. Topeka, KS: National Organization on Legal Problems of Education.

Hertz, R., & Imber, J. B. (Eds.). (1995). *Studying elites using qualitative methods.* Thousand Oaks, CA: Sage Publications.

Hill, M. E. (2002). Race of the interviewer and perception of skin color: Evidence from the multi-city study of urban inequality. *American Sociological Review, 67*(1), 99–108.

Holmes, S. L. (2004). An overview of African American college presidents: A game of two steps forward, one step backward, and standing still. *The Journal of Negro Education, 73*(1), 21–39.

Hoskins, R. L. (1978). *Black administrators in higher education: Conditions and perceptions.* New York: Praeger Publishers.

Jackson, J. F. L. (2001). A new test for diversity: Retaining African American administrators at predominantly white institutions. In L. Jones (Ed.), *Retaining African Americans in higher education: Challenging paradigms for retaining students, faculty, and administrators* (pp. 93–109). Sterling, VA: Stylus.

Jencks, C., & Riesman, D. (1967). The American Negro college. *Harvard Educational Review, 37*(1), 3–60.

Johnson, A. M. (1993). Bid, whist, tonk, and *United States v. Fordice*: Why integrationism fails African Americans again. *California Law Review, 81*, 1401–1470.

Johnson, B. J. (2001). Faculty socialization: Lessons learned from urban black colleges. *Urban Education, 36*(5), 630–647.

Johnson, B. J. (2004). Orientation and colleagues: Making a difference in the socialization of black college faculty. In. M. C. Brown & K. Freeman (Eds.), *Black colleges: New perspectives on policy and practice* (pp. 135–147). Westport, CT: Praeger.

Jones, M. H. (1971). The responsibility of the black college to the black community: Then and now. *Daedalus, 100*(1), 732–744.

June, A. W. (2003, January 17). Endangered institutions. *The Chronicle of Higher Education, 49*(19), A24.

Kannerstein, G. (1978). Black colleges: Self-concept. In C. V. Willie & R. R. Edmonds (Eds.), *Black colleges in America* (pp. 29–50). New York: Teachers College Press.

Kauffman, J. F. (1980). *At the pleasure of the board: The service of the college and university president.* Washington, DC: American Council on Education.

Krathwohl, D. R. (1998). *Methods of educational and social science research: An integrated approach* (2nd ed.). New York: Longman.

Kubala, T. S. (1999). A national study on the community college presidency. *Community College Journal of Research and Practice, 23*(2), 183–192.

Kuh, G. D., & Whitt, E. J. (1988). *The invisible tapestry: Culture in American colleges and universities.* ASHE-ERIC Higher Education Report, No. 1. Washington, DC: Association for the Study of Higher Education.

Kvale, S. (1996). *InterViews: An introduction to qualitative research interviewing.* Thousand Oaks, CA: Sage Publications.

Levinson, A. (2000). As different as day and night: Missouri's historically black Lincoln University, now predominantly white, searches for a way to bring its two divergent populations together. *Black Issues in Higher Education, 16*(23), 30–31.

Lewis, E. F. (1988). *The career development of black college presidents: A case of contest or sponsored mobility.* Unpublished dissertation, The Pennsylvania State University, University Park.

Lincoln, Y. S., & Guba, E. G. (1985). *Naturalistic inquiry.* Beverly Hills, CA: Sage.

Lindsay, B. (1998). Higher education policies and professional education in American black colleges. In K. Freeman (Ed.), *African American culture and heritage in higher education research and practice* (pp. 207–222). Westport, CT: Praeger.

Lindsay, B. (1999). Women chief executives and their approaches towards equity in American universities. *Comparative Education, 35,* 187–199.

Lofland, J., & Lofland, L. H. (1995). *Analyzing social settings: A guide to qualitative observation and analysis* (3rd ed.). Belmont, CA: Wadsworth Publishing Company.

Manning, K. (2000). *Rituals, ceremonies, and cultural meaning in higher education.* Westport, CT: Bergin & Garvey.

Masland, A. T. (1985). Organizational culture in the study of higher education. *Review of Higher Education, 8,* 157–168.

Maxwell, J. A. (1996). *Qualitative research design: An interactive approach.* Thousand Oaks, CA: Sage Publications.

Mays, B. (1978). The black college in higher education. In C. V. Willie & R. R. Edmonds (Eds.), *Black colleges in America* (pp. 19–28). New York: Teachers College Press.

McDonough, P. M., Antonio, A. L., & Trent, J. W. (1997). Black students, black colleges: An African American college choice model. *Journal for a Just and Caring Education, 3,* 9–36.

McFarlin, C. H., Crittenden, B. J, & Ebbers, L. H. (1999). Background factors common among outstanding community college presidents. *Community College Review, 27*(3), 19–32.

McMillan, J. H., & Schumacher, S. (1997). *Research in education: A conceptual introduction* (4th ed.). New York: Longman.

Moore, W., & Wagstaff, H. L. (1974). *Black educators in white colleges.* San Francisco: Jossey-Bass.

Moyser, G., & Wagstaff, M. (Eds.). (1987). *Research methods for elite studies.* London: Allen & Unwin.

Nettles, M. T. (1988). *Toward black undergraduate student equality in American higher education.* Westport, CT: Greenwood Press.

Outcalt, C. L., & Skewes-Cox, T. E. (2002). Involvement, interaction, and satisfaction: The human environment at HBCUs. *The Review of Higher Education, 25*(3), 331–347.

Patterson, C. (1994). Desegregation as a two-way street: The aftermath of *United States v. Fordice. Cleveland State Law Review, 42,* 377–434.

Peterson, M. W., & Spencer, M. G. (1990). Understanding academic culture and climate. In W. G. Tierney (Ed.), *Assessing academic climates and cultures* (pp. 3–18). New Directions for Institutional Research, No. 68. San Francisco: Jossey-Bass.

Phelps, D. G., Taber, L., & Smith, C. (1996). African American community college presidents. *Community College Review, 24*(4), 3–26.

Roebuck, J. B., & Murty, K. S. (1993). *Historically black colleges and universities: Their place in American higher education.* Westport, CT: Praeger.

Rolle, K. A., Davies, T. G., & Banning, J. H. (2000). African American administrators in predominantly white college and universities. *Community College Journal of Research and Practice, 24*(2), 79–94.

Ross, M., & Green, M. F. (2000). *The American college president: 2000 edition.* Washington, DC: American Council on Education.

Rubin, H. J., & Rubin, I. S. (2005). *Qualitative interviewing: The art of hearing data* (2nd ed.). Thousand Oaks, CA: Sage Publications.

Rudolph, F. (1962). *The American college and university: A history.* New York: Knopf.

Schein, E. H. (2004). *Organizational culture and leadership* (3rd ed.). San Francisco: Jossey-Bass.

Schwandt, T. A. (2001). *Dictionary of qualitative inquiry* (2nd ed.). Thousand Oaks, CA: Sage.

Scott, W. R. (1998). *Organizations: Rational, natural, and open systems* (4th ed.). Upper Saddle River, NJ: Prentice Hall.

Sims, S. J. (1994). *Diversifying historically black colleges and universities: A new higher education paradigm.* Westport, CT: Greenwood Press.

Slater, R. B. (1993). White professors at black colleges. *Journal of Blacks in Higher Education, 1*(1), 67–70.

Stark, J. S., & Lattuca, L. R. (1997). *Shaping the college curriculum: Academic plans in action.* Needham Heights, MA: Allyn & Bacon.

Thelin, J. R. (2004). *A history of American higher education.* Baltimore, MD: The Johns Hopkins University Press.

Thomas, R. J. (1995). Interviewing important people in big companies. In R. Hertz & J. B. Imber (Eds.), *Studying elites using qualitative methods* (pp. 3–17). Thousand Oaks, CA: Sage.

Thompson, C. (1998). Historical origins of change: Implications for African Americans in higher education. In K. Freeman (Ed.), *African American culture and heritage in higher education research and practice* (pp. 43–53). Westport, CT: Praeger.

Thompson, D. C. (1978). Black college faculty and students: The nature of their interaction. In C. V. Willie & R. R. Edmonds (Eds.), *Black colleges in America* (pp. 180–194). New York: Teachers College Press.

Tierney, W. G. (1988). Organizational culture in higher education. *Journal of Higher Education, 59*(1), 2–21.

Turner, C., & Myers, S. (2000). *Faculty of color in academe: Bittersweet success.* Needham Heights, MA: Allyn and Bacon.

Vaughan, G. B., & Weisman, I. M. (1997). Selected characteristics of community college trustees and presidents. *New Directions for Community Colleges, 25*(2), 5–12.

Veysey, L. R. (1965). *The emergence of the American university.* Chicago: University of Chicago Press.

Walters, R. (1991). *A cultural strategy for the survival of historically black colleges and universities.* Paper presented at the annual conference of the National Council for Black Studies, Atlanta, GA.

Weick, K. E. (1995). *Sensemaking in organizations.* Thousand Oaks, CA: Sage.

Wenglinsky, H. (1997). *Students at historically black colleges and universities: Their aspirations and accomplishments.* Princeton, NJ: Educational Testing Service.

Williams, J. (Ed.). (1988). *Desegregating America's colleges and universities: Title VI regulation of higher education.* New York: Teachers College Press.

Willie, C. V. (1981a, January). Make it possible for whites to be the minority: An educational goal for the next twenty-five years. *Negro Educational Review, 32,* 78–88.

Willie, C. V. (1981b). *The ivory and ebony towers.* Lexington, MA: Lexington Books.

Willie, C. V. (1994). Black colleges are not just for blacks anymore. *Journal of Negro Education, 63*(2), 153–163.

Willie, C. V., & MacLeish, M. Y. (1978). The priorities of presidents of black colleges. In C. V. Willie & R. R. Edmonds (Eds.), *Black colleges in America* (pp. 132–148). New York: Teachers College Press.

Zemsky, R., Wegner, G. R., & Massy, W. F. (2005). *Remaking the American university: Market-smart and mission-centered.* New Brunswick, NJ: Rutgers University Press.

# Four-Year, Historically Black Colleges and Universities

## Alabama

1. Alabama A & M University (public)
2. Alabama State University (public)
3. Miles College (private)
4. Oakwood College (private)
5. Selma University (private)
6. Stillman College (private)
7. Talladega College (private)
8. Tuskegee University (private)

## Arkansas

9. Arkansas Baptist College (private)
10. Philander Smith College (private)
11. University of Arkansas at Pine Bluff (public)

## Delaware

12. Delaware State University (public)

## District of Columbia

13. Howard University (private)
14. University of the District of Columbia (public)

## Florida

15. Bethune-Cookman College (private)
16. Edward Waters College (private)
17. Florida A & M University (public)
18. Florida Memorial College (private)

# Georgia

19. Albany State College (public)
20. Clark Atlanta University (private)
21. Fort Valley State College (public)
22. Interdenominational Theological Center (private)
23. Morehouse College (private)
24. Morehouse School of Medicine (private)
25. Morris Brown College (private)
26. Paine College (private)
27. Savannah State College (public)
28. Spelman College (private)

# Kentucky

29. Kentucky State University (public)

# Louisiana

30. Dillard University (private)
31. Grambling State University (public)
32. Southern University A & M College—Baton Rouge (public)
33. Southern University at New Orleans (public)
34. Xavier University of Louisiana (private)

# Maryland

35. Bowie State University (public)
36. Coppin State University (public)
37. Morgan State University (public)
38. University of Maryland–Eastern Shore (public)

# Mississippi

39. Alcorn State University (public)
40. Jackson State University (public)
41. Mississippi Valley State University (public)

42. Rust College (private)
43. Tougaloo College (private)

## Missouri

44. Harris-Stowe State College (public)
45. Lincoln University (public)

## North Carolina

46. Barber-Scotia College (private)
47. Bennett College (private)
48. Elizabeth City State University (public)
49. Fayetteville State University (public)
50. Johnson C. Smith University (private)
51. Livingstone College (private)
52. North Carolina A & T State University (public)
53. North Carolina Central University (public)
54. St. Augustine's College (private)
55. Shaw University (private)
56. Winston-Salem State University (public)

## Ohio

57. Central State University (public)
58. Wilberforce University (private)

## Oklahoma

59. Langston University (public)

## Pennsylvania

60. Cheyney State University (public)
61. Lincoln University (public)

## South Carolina

62. Allen University (private)
63. Benedict College (private)
64. Claflin College (private)
65. Morris College (private)
66. South Carolina State University (public)
67. Voorhees College (private)

## Tennessee

68. Fisk University (private)
69. Knoxville College (private)
70. Lane College (private)
71. LeMoyne-Owen College (private)
72. Meharry Medical College (private)
73. Tennessee State University (public)

## Texas

74. Huston-Tillotson College (private)
75. Jarvis Christian College (private)
76. Paul Quinn College (private)
77. Prairie View A & M University (public)
78. Southwestern Christian College (private)
79. Texas College (private)
80. Texas Southern University (public)
81. Wiley College (private)

## Virginia

82. Hampton University (private)
83. Norfolk State University (public)
84. Saint Paul's College (private)
85. Virginia State University (public)
86. Virginia Union University (private)

## West Virginia

87. Bluefield State College (public)
88. West Virginia State University (public)

## U.S. Virgin Islands

89. University of the Virgin Islands (public)

# Predominantly Black Colleges and Universities

## Alabama

1. Wallace Community College-Sparks Campus (public; two-year)
2. John M. Patterson State Technical College (public; two-year)
3. Reid State Technical College (public; two-year)

## California

4. Charles R. Drew University of Medicine and Science (private; four-year)
5. Compton Community College (public; two-year)
6. Los Angeles Southwest College (public; two-year)
7. West Los Angeles College (public; two-year)

## District of Columbia

8. Southeastern University (private; four-year)

## Georgia

9. Albany Technical Institute (public; two-year)
10. Atlanta Metropolitan College (public; two-year)
11. Bauder College (private; two-year)
12. Central Georgia Technical College (public; two-year)
13. Columbus Technical College (public; two-year)
14. DeKalb Technical College (public; two-year)
15. Georgia Military College-Augusta-Fort Gordon Campus (public; two-year)
16. Georgia Military College-Fort McPherson Campus (public; two-year)
17. Gupton Jones College of Funeral Service (public; two-year)

18. Herzing College-Atlanta (private; four-year)
19. Savannah Technical College (public; two-year)

## Illinois

20. Chicago State University (public; four-year)
21. East St. Louis Community College (public; two-year)
22. East-West University (private; four-year)
23. Kennedy-King College (public; two-year)
24. Malcolm X College (public; two-year)
25. Olive-Harvey College (public; two-year)

## Indiana

26. Martin University (private; four-year)

## Kentucky

27. Simmons University [Bible College] (private; four-year)

## Maryland

28. Baltimore City Community College (public; two-year)
29. Prince George's Community College (public; two-year)
30. Sojourner-Douglass College (private; four-year)

## Massachusetts

31. Roxbury Community College (public; two-year)

## Michigan

32. Davenport University-Dearborn (private; four-year)
33. Davenport University-Flint (private; four-year)
34. Wayne County Community College (public; two-year)

## Mississippi

35.  East Mississippi Community College (public; two-year)
36.  Mississippi Delta Community College (public; two-year)
37.  Natchez Junior College (private; two-year)

## New Jersey

38.  Bloomfield College (private; four-year)
39.  Essex County College (public; two-year)

## New York

40.  Audrey Cohen College (private; four-year)
41.  Fiorello H. LaGuardia (public; two-year)
42.  Helene Fuld College of Nursing of North General Hospital (private; two-year)
43.  Long Island College Hospital School of Nursing (private; two-year)
44.  Medgar Evers College (public; four-year)
45.  New York City Technical College (public; two-year)
46.  York College (public; four-year)

## North Carolina

47.  Edgecombe Community College (public; two-year)
48.  Roanoke-Chowan Community College (public; two-year)

## Ohio

49.  Cuyahoga Community College (public; two-year)

## Pennsylvania

50.  Peirce College (private; four-year)

## South Carolina

51.  Williamsburg Technical College (public; two-year)

## Tennessee

    52. Southwest Tennessee Community College (public; two-year)

## Texas

    53. Bay Ridge Christian College (private; two-year)

## Virginia

    54. Virginia University at Lynchburg (private; four-year)

## U.S. Virgin Islands

    55. University of the Virgin Islands (public; four-year)

# The Research Framework: A Note on Method

This is a qualitative study that uses elite interviewing to explore how presidents of four-year historically Black colleges and universities define and implement the mission of their respective institutions. The objective is to move beyond the confines of traditional mission statements to gain a deeper understanding of the role of Black colleges in the larger system of higher education. The study targeted presidents because as chief executive officers they have comprehensive authority over and responsibility for the institutions; therefore, they are most qualified to address the topic of mission.

The following questions guide the research: How do presidents of four-year historically Black colleges and universities define the mission of their institutions? How do presidents of four-year historically Black colleges and universities implement the mission of their institutions? What do presidents of four-year historically Black colleges and universities identify as significant barriers to mission implementation? This appendix, which details the research methods used for the study, is divided into six sections: (a) qualitative research, (b) conceptual framework, (c) population and sample, (d) data collection, (e) data analysis, and (f) limitations of the research.

## Qualitative Research

The study uses qualitative research methods due to the nature of the questions posed. According to Schwandt (2001), qualitative inquiry, "aims at understanding the meaning of human inquiry"(p. 213). McMillan & Schumacher (1997) echo this sentiment and offer the following: "Qualitative research is concerned with understanding the social phenomenon from the participants' perspective. Understanding is acquired by analyzing the many contexts of the participants and by narrating participants' meanings for these situations and events. Participants' meanings include their feelings, beliefs, ideals, thoughts, and actions" (p. 392).

According to Denzin and Lincoln (2000), two of the foremost authorities on the method of qualitative research,

Qualitative research is a situated activity that locates the observer in the world. It consists of a set of interpretive, material practices that make the world visible. These practices transform the world. They turn the world into a series of representations, including field notes, interviews, conversations, photographs, recordings, and memos to the self. At this level, qualitative research involves an interpretive, naturalistic approach to the world. This means that qualitative researchers study things in their natural settings, attempting to make sense of, or to interpret, phenomena in terms of the meanings people bring to them. (p. 3)

Despite the various definitions of qualitative research, all of the authors' interpretations coincide with Bogdan and Biklen's (1998) identification of five features of qualitative inquiry, which include naturalistic, descriptive, concern with process, inductive, and meaning. Situating the study within the context of qualitative method provides the researcher an opportunity to gain an in-depth understanding of how presidents of historically Black colleges and universities make sense of their campuses. The primary focus is on quality, a word that identifies with the nature or essence of something. The qualitative approach is particularly useful because it creates a platform to give a voice to Black college presidents, a voice that remains relatively silent in the academic literature.

## Elite Interviewing

Interviews are conversations with structure and purpose (Kvale, 1996) that can elicit multiple perspectives on a given topic (Rubin & Rubin, 2005). An elite interview focuses on participants who hold important and highly selective positions of authority and influence. The study used the qualitative technique of elite interviewing as the means to better understand the mission of Black colleges from an insider's perspective. The president serves as the ultimate insider because he or she is responsible for all facets of campus operations. Presidents are elites because they occupy the most powerful position on campus as the highest-ranking administrator. The biggest challenge in studying an elite group of people is gaining access to them (Dexter, 1970; Hertz & Imber, 1995; Moyser & Wagstaffe, 1987; Thomas, 1995). The process of acquiring access to participants and establishing a relationship with them is a critical component of qualitative research (Bogdan & Biklen, 1998; Krathwohl, 1998; Lofland & Lofland, 1995; Maxwell, 1996). According to

Thomas (1995), elites are visible but not accessible. Perhaps this challenge helps to explain the lack of studies, particularly qualitative studies, on presidents of historically Black institutions of higher education.

## Symbolic Interactionism

The qualitative research study is situated within the interpretive tradition of symbolic interactionism. According to Schwandt (2001), this social psychological theory stems primarily from the works of George Hebert Mead and Hebert Blumer. Symbolic interactionism suggests that people construct meaning through social interactions. Although the act of making meaning is subjective, the process of interacting helps individuals to develop common definitions or shared perspectives (Bogdan & Biklen, 1998). For purposes of the study, symbolic interaction recognizes the role of the president and the environment in which he or she resides. Although presidents are elites, mission making is not an isolated process. Presidents are able to understand their campuses through their interactions with students, faculty, staff, administrators, and the surrounding community.

## Conceptual Framework

The framework for the study is embedded primarily in higher education organization and governance. A helpful way to understand how colleges and universities work is to view them as organizations (Birnbaum, 1988a; Bolman & Deal, 1997). Institutions of higher education represent what Scott (1998) describes as an open system organization. An open system consists of individuals with varied responsibilities who contribute to the collective mission on an organization. According to Scott (1998), "the open system perspective stresses the reciprocal ties that bind and relate the organization with those elements that surround and penetrate it" (p. 100). The term *governance* refers to "the structures and processes through which institutional participants interact with and influence each other and communicate with the larger environment" (Birnbaum, 1988a, p. 4). Organization and governance provide a useful foundation for analyzing the mission of historically Black colleges and universities because it highlights that institutions of higher education are multilayered organizations, and the way in which they are governed varies across campuses. The assertion is not that Black colleges operate in a different structural manner from other types of higher education institutions, but, rather, certain issues should be considered when attempting to examine them because of the population they primarily serve and their historical development. Additionally, all historically Black colleges and universities are not the same, and the assumption is that the presidents' perspectives on mission will vary from one campus to the next. The purpose of this framework is to highlight the following considerations that guide the study: (a) sensemaking, (b) organizational culture and context, and (c) contingency theory.

## *Sensemaking*

The mission of a college or university defines its overall function, objective, and contribution. Although mission appears to be a fundamental component of any organization, creating, understanding, and articulating a sense of purpose is a complex process (Cohen & March, 1986; Hartley, 2002). Colleges and universities have numerous responsibilities. They are expected to provide an academic foundation, encourage social awareness, build character, increase understanding, cultivate tolerance, shape morals, and, ultimately, mold the minds of young people. The problem is that institutions of higher education attempt to be all things to all people, and, as a result, the basic topic of mission gets lost in the shuffle of other responsibilities. This problem does not negate the importance of understanding mission; rather, it calls attention to the fact that discourse on this topic is needed, particularly for historically Black colleges and universities.

Karl E. Weick (1995), an expert on organizational behavior, proposes using sensemaking as a framework to aid in examining the dynamics of organizations. Sensemaking literally means to make sense of something. In the case of organizations, sensemaking is concerned with the ways in which individuals generate interpretations and construct meaning. Sensemaking is about processing, organizing, and transforming the subjective into something concrete. Sensemaking shapes organizational structure and influences behavior.

The seven features that best characterize sensemaking include (a) grounded in identity construction, (b) retrospective, (c) enactive of sensible environments, (d) social, (e) ongoing, (f) focused on and extracted by cues, and (g) driven by plausibility rather than accuracy (Weick, 1995). Identity construction implies that sensemaking involves an individual, or a sense-maker. The sensemaker's identity represents his or her role within an organization and is constructed based on interactions with other people and the environment in which the sensemaker is situated. The retrospective feature of sensemaking offers that "people can know what they are doing only after they have done it" (Weick, 1995, p. 24). The creation of meaning requires attention and deliberate effort, and it can be accomplished only after something has been lived or experienced. Individuals are more cognizant of what they have done than they are of what they are doing.

The evidence of sensible environments characteristic of sensemaking indicates that people help to create the environments of which they are a part. The environment is not a distant entity, and sensemaking forces individuals to recognize that they are the environment because the contributions they make ultimately shape and structure it. The social aspect of sensemaking simply suggests that the process does not occur in isolation. Sensemaking involves a sense of community, interaction, shared meanings, and common language and symbols. The reference to sensemaking as ongoing indicates that it is a never-ending process because individuals are in a constant state of being. The need to extract cues from sensemaking suggests that, because people are able to make sense out of every situation, it is important to help direct their attention. This feature of sensemaking is particularly helpful for researchers as they must provide the proper context to obtain relevant information from the sensemaker. Sensemaking should not be a meaningless process, nor should it be driven by accuracy. According to Weick (1995), "sensemaking is about plausibility, pragmatics, coherence, reasonableness, creation, invention, and instrumentality" (p. 57). Individuals experience and interpret the world in varied ways, and each of their respective truths is valuable.

Why is sensemaking an important consideration for the study of the mission of historically Black colleges and universities? Black institutions of higher education, more than other types of postsecondary schools, consistently face questions about their worth. Many people opposed the mere development of these schools, and, as a result, these institutions continue to struggle with justifying their place within the larger higher education system. The sensemaking lens provides an opportunity to attempt to answer the critics who are skeptical of the purpose that Black colleges serve. Drawing from Weick's (1995) explanation of sensemaking, here is an explanation of how the research study aligns with the seven aforementioned characteristics and how it uses this ontological framework as a guiding lens.

For the purpose of the study, the presidents of four-year historically Black colleges and universities serve as the sensemaker. As the chief executive officers, they remain abreast of all university operations, so they are qualified to retrospectively make sense of the mission of their respective institutions. Presidents are an integral part of the campus environment and play key roles in structuring the overall objectives. They do not act in isolation, however, and they recognize the value of the social aspect of sensemaking. Board members, other administrators, faculty, staff, students, and the surrounding communities influence and contribute to ongoing decision making that affects the schools. The intent of the study is to extract cues only on the topic of mission and enable presidents of historically Black colleges and universities to share their perspectives and tell their stories concerning the purpose of their institutions.

## Organizational Culture and Context

Organizational culture represents a critical component of any organization, particularly colleges and universities. Researchers suggest that any attempt to thoroughly understand how organizations work, begins with an examination of the culture (Clark, 1972; Kuh & Whitt, 1988; Masland, 1985; Peterson & Spencer, 1990; Schein, 2004). Edgar H. Schein, a pioneer in psychology, has created an extensive body of work focusing on the dynamics of organizations. In his most recent book, *Organizational Culture and Leadership*, Schein (2004) insists that, when individuals attempt to study and analyze any type of organization, they must use a cultural lens. The concept of culture is complex because the word encompasses a multitude of meanings. Culture identifies a way of life, an attitude or behavior characteristic of a particular organization or social group. Culture is the invisible tapestry (Kuh & Whitt, 1988) that induces purpose and provides meaning (Masland, 1985). Culture is synonymous with words such as values, beliefs, rituals, norms, traditions, and background.

According to Schein (2004), the four key characteristics that distinguish culture from other terms are structural stability, depth, breadth, and patterning or integration. Structural stability means that culture is resilient and firmly established. This stability plays a major role in contributing to the overall identity of the organization. Culture is powerful in that as individuals matriculate in and out of organizations, the culture remains intact. Depth, which implies that culture is the foundation of any organization, consists of the intangibles that may not be visible to the naked eye, yet it represents the fabric of the organization that is readily felt. Breadth signifies the influential power of culture. Culture affects every aspect of a functioning organization. Finally, the patterning or integration characteristic involves merging the synonymous words (traditions, norms, background, values, beliefs, and rituals) into what is identified as culture. Culture is all-encompassing, and understanding it enables individuals to engage in what Weick (1995) identifies as sensemaking.

Culture is a familiar term, yet it remains abstract. This abstractness contributes to the ongoing need to define, articulate, and measure what culture truly is. Perhaps the most intriguing aspect of culture as a concept is that it "directs us to phenomena that are below the surface, that are powerful in their impact but invisible and, to a considerable degree, unconscious. In that sense, culture is to a group what personality or character is to an individual. We can see the behavior that results, but often we cannot see the forces underneath that cause certain kinds of behavior" (Schein, 2004, p. 8).

Historically Black colleges and universities pose a similar kind of curiosity. Since their inception, such institutions have struggled to compete with the prestige, power, and resources afforded to majority-White schools. The reality is that Black colleges were founded on the premise of separate and unequal, and they received less funding merely to maintain their campuses. As a result, these schools were left with less of everything. Indeed, Black colleges have made significant progress, but they continue to fight for respect as viable higher education institutions. The irony is that, despite the shortcomings of Black colleges and universities, they persevere. The key question is, *how?* How can Black colleges attract so many students when they do not have the beautiful campus facilities of majority schools? How are historically Black colleges able to enroll students with learning deficiencies, graduate them, and send a significant number off to graduate and professional schools? How is it that North Carolina A& T State University is the leading producer of African American baccalaureates in engineering? How can Xavier University of Louisiana place more African Americans into medical school than any other school in the nation? With the majority of African American students attending predominantly White colleges, how is it that historically Black colleges and universities remain the undergraduate home of most African American federal judges, medical doctors, army officers, and doctoral degree recipients (Brown, 2002a).

Fleming (1984) offers that the mystique surrounding historically Black colleges and universities stems partly from an inability to measure the intangible services they provide. The service of a nurturing campus environment or the provision of supportive faculty, for example, contributes to the ongoing achievement of students, yet these intangibles remain difficult to quantify. The inability to measure such services place Black colleges and universities at a considerable disadvantage in regard to the research community because the value of these services often goes unnoticed. Although a sense of wonder surrounds historically Black colleges and the concept of culture, both undeniably perform a necessary function within the larger system of higher education.

In *African American Culture and Heritage in Higher Education Research and Practice*, Kassie Freeman (1998) identifies herself an African American storyteller of higher education research and raises a critical question: "Why is it imperative to consider culture and heritage in academic research and policymaking?" The problem, in her opinion, is that the real educational stories of Black people are not depicted properly in academic research. Numerous studies target African Americans, but researchers often neglect to consider the culture and history of Black people. This view coincides with Brown's (2003) assertion that one of the fallacies concerning research on Black colleges is that most of the work is approached from an *etic*, or distant, perspective. Investigators remain outsiders because they conduct research through observation and fail to engage fully in, or merely consider, the culture of the Black college campus. An outsider is not limited only to non-African American investigators, but rather, all researchers who fail to situate their study within a culturally sensitive framework. The absence of this consideration contributes to the plethora of inadequate stories told of the African American learning experience that dominate the field of education under the guise of reputable academic research.

The challenge is that improper assessment breeds improper solutions. To remedy this problem, Freeman (1998) proposes the need for a cultural context framework. She writes:

> Cultural context, then, can be defined as interrelated characteristics that provide a perspective—frame of reference—for understanding individuals'

and/or groups' ways of knowing and being. These interrelated characteristics generally include the sum total of the makeup of individuals. By way of example, cultural context is to the individual as conceptual framework is to research. When either is missing, the purpose, clarity of meaning, or sense of direction seems to be unclear or lost. (p. 2)

Consideration of cultural context is imperative for research on historically Black colleges and universities. All higher education institutions have some degree of culture embedded in them. They possess their own language, symbols, rituals, traditions, and ceremonies (Manning, 2000), which affect sensemaking (Weick, 1995). Black colleges, however, receive regular recognition and, often, praise for providing a campus culture that is unique and empowering for African American students (Brown, 2002a; Fleming, 1984; Garibaldi, 1984; Roebuck & Murty, 1993). The framework of cultural context forces the researcher to acknowledge that historically Black colleges and universities have a distinct organizational culture as a group of institutions united in the historic mission of providing educational opportunities for African American students. In addition, all Black colleges are different, and each one has its own sense of culture. Examining historically Black colleges and universities, for purposes of the study, requires deliberate consideration of culture and its influence on presidential perspectives on defining mission.

## Contingency Theory

Contingency theory operates primarily within an open system perspective that suggests that the environment plays a critical role in deciding the manner in which an organization functions (Scott, 1998; Tierney, 1988). Such theory suggests that different situations require different patterns of behavior and traits (Bensimon, Neumann, & Birnbaum, 1989).

In an influential work, *A Theory of Leadership Effectiveness*, Fiedler (1967) introduces the contingency model and asserts that effectiveness depends on the relationship between leadership style and the extent to which the situation allows the leader to exert influence over group members. In this particular context, leadership style refers to a personality factor that causes a leader to be either task-oriented or relationship-oriented. Leaders who are task-oriented tend to approach leadership in the traditional sense: they take charge and direct group members. Conversely, relationship-oriented leaders approach leadership in a more cooperative manner by inviting group members to share decision-making responsibilities. The situation addressed in the contingency theory refers to characteristics of the particular environment in which the leader is located.

Fiedler (1967) proposes consideration of three important situational factors: (a) the leader's position power, (b) the structure of the task, and (c) the interpersonal relationship between leaders and other members of the organization. Position power is the extent to which the position itself authorizes leaders to control the direction of the organization by convincing group members to accept and follow their leadership. Task structure refers to the degree to which group members are given clear goals and expectations regarding their assigned job. The interpersonal relationship between leaders and members, perhaps the most important of all three factors, reflects the amount of support group members provide to their leaders based on the leaders' personality and work history within the organization.

The fundamental premise of contingency theory is that leadership varies, depending on the demands of the external environment (Birnbaum, 1988b). To be effective, leaders must find a favorable fit within an organization. According to Fiedler (1967), a leader who performs well under one set of conditions does not necessarily translate into an effective leader in another situation. Contingency theory is relevant to the study of Black college presidents because it validates the need for a more specialized focus for the college presidency. The traditional method of investigating college presidents consists of educators acquiring the perspectives of leaders of different institutional types, ranging from large, research institutions to small, liberal arts colleges. While this approach is helpful in that it incorporates the experiences of a diverse group of presidents, findings are presented in such a way that the value of the varying perspectives is lost. The concept of leadership is projected as a consensus because the gathered information is synthesized to the detriment of uncovering the individuality of the presidents based on the various kinds of institutions they lead. This method is particularly problematic for presidents of Black colleges because these leaders are often excluded from larger studies of the college presidency. As a result, their leadership experience is neither considered nor documented. Contingency theory acknowledges the need to understand the dynamics of leadership and how leaders vary according to the situation in which they are placed.

Contingency theory is appropriate for the study because it calls attention to the Black college environment, recognizing that Black schools are a diverse group of institutions, and how presidents define mission is contingent on numerous factors. Brown (2003) states that the mission of Black colleges is contingent on time, place, and circumstance. Based on the tenets of contingency theory, the mission of Black institutions is not a universal standard, and presidents define mission based on the values and priorities deemed important by the institution they lead. The assumption of the study is that, although Black colleges are not homogenous institutions, they do share an organizational culture that differs significantly from mainstream higher education. The overall cultural context of the Black college campus influences how presidents make sense of their institutions.

## Population and Sample

The overall population of the study consists of presidents of four-year colleges and universities federally designated as historically Black institutions of higher education (see Appendix A). The American higher education institution includes 89 four-year, historically Black colleges and universities (Brown, 2002a; Brown et al., 2004; Coaxum, 2001; Fleming, 1984; Garibaldi, 1984; Roebuck & Murty, 1993). The study used purposive (or purposeful) sampling, which consists of strategically selecting participants based on their ability to provide optimal insight in regard to the focus of a research study (Creswell 1998; Fraenkel & Wallen, 2003; Krathwohl 1998; Maxwell, 1996; McMillan & Schumacher, 1997; Schwandt, 2001). The complete population of 89 four-year, historically Black college presidents was invited to participate in the study in an effort to attain more representative results. A total of 15 presidents completed the project, yielding approximately 16.85% of the population of four-year, historically Black college and university presidents.

The strength of this research study lies in the size of the sample compared to existing studies on presidents of historically Black colleges and universities. The American Council on Education produces a series of reports on the national corpus of college and university presidents whose demographic database is a popular source of information as it details the presidents' length of service, age, educational background, and a host of other characteristics (Ross & Green, 2000). While the information is statistically precise and empirically rigorous, masked within these facts are the place and future of Black college presidents. In Buchanan's (1988) study of the roles and qualifications of Black college presidents, the researcher completed 12 interviews with presidents, academic vice presidents, and senior faculty members; only four presidents participated in the study. Holmes (2004) examined the career path of African American presidents. The researchers interviewed six presidents, but the results remain unclear about how many of many were presidents of historically Black colleges. This research study, however, provides in-depth examination of the mission of historically Black colleges from 16.85% of the total population of four-year presidents of Black colleges, thus making it the largest collection of data on Black college presidents to date.

## Data Collection

The effort to recruit participants for the study occurred in five phases due to the challenge of gaining access to elites. First, participant solicitation began with researchers drafting a request letter and mailing copies to the campus addresses of the entire population of 89 four-year, historically Black college and university presidents. The letter, whose intent was to convince the presidents that the research would make a meaningful contribution to the field of higher education, succinctly explained the purpose and significance of the study. Hill (2002) contends that the race of the interviewer influences the interview process. As a result, the single researcher who conducted all interviews therefore revealed her identity as an African American graduate of a historically Black school as a means to gain access (Bogdan & Biklen, 1998) to chief academic officers. Second, the researchers sent an electronic copy of the official letter directly to the presidents or the executive assistants to the presidents, provided the schools' home websites disclosed this information. Third, the researchers attended the 2005 White House Initiative on Historically Black Colleges and Universities conference held in Washington, D.C. Many Black college presidents participated in the conference, coincidently titled, *The Mission Continues*. Next, the researchers traveled to New Orleans, Louisiana, to attend the annual 2006 National Association for Equal Opportunity in Higher Education (NAFEO) conference on African Americans in higher education. Finally, the researchers made personal phone calls to the presidents' offices to encourage them to get involved with the study.

In addition to the five phases, the researchers used the snowball sampling technique. In qualitative research, snowball sampling occurs when one participant encourages another individual to engage in the research study (Bogdan & Biklen, 1998). The researchers made deliberate efforts to recruit a representative and diverse sample of presidents and institutions. In regard to the presidents, the researchers tried to acquire adequate representation of women and presidents who have held both short- and long-term tenures. Historically Black colleges and universities are a diverse cohort of institutions, so the researchers made every attempt to include institutions that varied in size, sector, and geographic location.

Before the interviews, participating presidents received a letter of informed consent explaining that participation in the study was strictly voluntary, and the responses would remain confidential. Confidentiality is critical, particularly when interviewing elites such as college presidents. The researchers informed the presidents that pseudonyms would be used in place of their names and the names of their respective schools. In addition to the letter of informed consent, the presidents received a copy of the interview questions. Again, because presidents are part of an elite class, this courtesy was extended so they would understand the nature of the research study.

The telephone interviews lasted approximately 35 to 60 minutes. A total of 14 presidents granted the researchers permission to record the interviews, and one (1) asked not to be audiotaped. The semistructured interview protocol consisted of three categories of questions. The first set served as a warm-up by including getting-to-know-you-better questions. These questions centered on the presidents' personal background and their journey toward their position. Specific research questions, which made up the second category, steered the presidents' attention directly to their institutions and their role in them. The third category asked questions about Black colleges as a whole to obtain presidential perspectives on the current and future state of all historically Black colleges and universities based on their experiences as leaders of these institutions.

The researchers offered to send all of the participants a copy of the interview transcripts on the completion of the telephone interviews. Lincoln and Guba (1985) refer to this process as member check. Offering transcribed interviews was meant to ensure the accuracy of the interviews by allowing the presidents an opportunity to examine and provide feedback on the communication. Only one president accepted this offer.

## Data Analysis

The researchers transcribed all of the information gathered from the interviews with the 14 presidents and the notes from the 1 untaped president, primarily to ensure the accuracy of the information. However, transcribing the interviews also allowed the researcher to become immersed in the data, which helped in the coding process. Each interview was transcribed on the day it took place to manage the large volume of data. The researchers identified emerging themes from the data throughout the interview and transcription process. As the presidents offered their perspectives on the mission of Black colleges, both common and divergent themes emerged. The information was coded and analyzed based on the identified themes.

## Limitations of the Research

The limitations of the study include:

1. The study focuses only on four-year, historically Black colleges, not predominantly Black colleges and universities or other minority-serving institutions. Predominantly Black institutions refers to colleges and universities with a greater than 50% African American student population (see Appendix B).
2. Although the study represents the highest percentage of historically Black college and university presidents included in a research study, it does not provide the generalizability that unanimous participation would.
3. The fact that the researchers conducted all of the interviews by telephone may have influenced how the presidents responded to the questions and how much information they disclosed. The presidents in the study may have been more comfortable talking with either of the two researchers if a relationship had been established through personal contact.

**Ronyelle Bertrand Ricard** received her Ed.M. in higher education administration from the University of Illinois at Urbana-Champaign and her Ph.D. in higher education with a cognate in sociology from The Pennsylvania State University. She currently serves as coordinator of Middle States Self-Study in the Office of the President at Howard University. Before assuming her current position, Dr. Ricard was coordinator of Research and Professional Development at the American Association of Colleges for Teacher Education. She also completed a research internship at the Frederick D. Patterson Research Institute of the United Negro College Fund. Dr. Ricard's research interests and publications focus on access, organizational theory, presidential leadership, and historically Black colleges and universities.

Dr. Ricard has published articles, essays, or reviews in *The Journal of Higher Education, Urban Education*, and *NACADA Journal*. She also co-authored a chapter, "The Changing Role of Historically Black Colleges and Universities: Vistas on Dual Missions, Desegregation, and Diversity" in *Black Colleges: New Perspectives on Policy and Practice*. She has completed a national study of publication trends in *The Review of Higher Education*, she is now involved in a national study of African American college presidents in both historically Black- and majority-White-enrolled colleges and universities.

**M. Christopher Brown II** received his Ph.D. in higher education with cognates in public administration and political science from The Pennsylvania State University. Currently professor and dean of the College of Education at the University of Nevada, Las Vegas, he previously served as vice president for programs and administration at the American Association of Colleges for Teacher Education, director of social justice and professional development for the American Educational Research Association (AERA), and executive director and chief research scientist of the Frederick D. Patterson Research Institute of the United Negro College Fund. Dr. Brown has held faculty appointments at The Pennsylvania State University, the University of Illinois at Urbana-Champaign, and the University of Missouri-Kansas City. Dr. Brown earned a national reputation for his research and scholarly writing on higher education policy and administration, meriting him both the Association for the Study of Higher Education (ASHE) (2001) and AERA (2002) early career research awards. His research addresses higher education leadership and governance, postsecondary statutory and legal concerns, institutional history, and collegiate diversity. This scholarly agenda focuses on increasing effectiveness and efficiency, building organizational capacity, and assessing outcomes in campus settings. Dr. Brown is especially well known for his studies of historically Black colleges, educational equity, and institutional culture. He has written/edited numerous books and monographs and has published more than 90 journal articles, book chapters, and scholarly publications related to education and society. Dr. Brown has received research support from the Lumina Foundation, Spencer Foundation, AT&T Foundation, the Pew Charitable Trusts, the Sallie Mae Fund, and other foundations and corporations. He has lectured and/or presented scholarship in various countries in Africa, Asia, Australia, Europe, and North and South America